Judy Moody Goes to Hollywood

Behind the Scenes with Judy Moody and Friends

by Megan McDonald
with Richard Haynes
set photography by Suzanne Tenner

WALKER
BOOKS

First published 2011 by Walker Books Ltd
87 Vauxhall Walk, London SE11 5HJ

2 4 6 8 10 9 7 5 3 1

Based on the theatrical motion picture *Judy Moody and the NOT Bummer Summer*, produced by Smokewood Entertainment Group, LLC

This book has been typeset in Stone Informal and Judy Moody

Printed in Melrose Park, IL, USA

British Library Cataloguing in Publication Data: a catalogue record for
this book is available from the British Library

ISBN 978-1-4063-3594-1

www.walker.co.uk

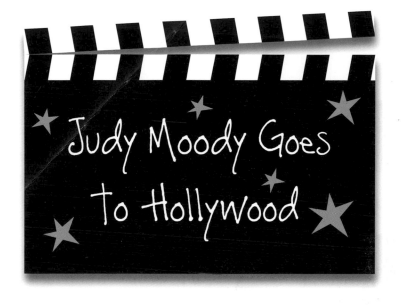

Judy Moody Goes to Hollywood

Above: Megan McDonald and Jordana Beatty
Opposite page: Garrett Ryan, Jordana Beatty, Taylar Hender, Preston Bailey

For Sarah

Judy Moody Gets Famous— for Real!

"IN A HOLLYWOOD MOOD"
by Judy Moody

Hey, everybody! I, Judy Moody, have some way-rare, mega-exciting news. Thrill-o-rama! You know how I've been trying to get famous for a while now? First it was a picture of my elbow in the newspaper. Then they spelled my name *Judy Muddy*. I thought I'd never ever EVER get famous.

But, guess what! There's now a movie all about—you guessed it—me, me, me, me, ME! For sure and absolute positive. It's called *Judy Moody and the NOT Bummer Summer*.

I, and nobody else but me, got the top-secret, WAY-behind-the-scenes inside poop-scoop about the making of the whole, entire movie. It's so uber-awesome I just had to give you a peek! From bike chases to Bigfoot races, tightropes to high hopes for the best summer ever—it's all here! Start turning the pages and earn thrill points as you go. One word says it all:

Super-cali-fragi-listic-expi-thrilla-delic!

THE MANY MOODS OF JUDY MOODY

Excited about a summer of thrills ahead. Down in the dumps when she has to say so long to her best friend. From mad moods to glad moods to sad moods, Judy Moody has felt them all. In fact, Judy has so many moods, it's like taking a ride on the Scream Monster roller coaster at Scare Devil Island Amusement Park!

* Happy
* Glad

* Unhappy
* Sad

* Grouchy
* Impossible

* Jealous
* Envy

* Curious
* Eager

* Frustrated
* Mad

* Joyful
* On Top of the World

WHO'S WHO

Finding the right actors and actresses to bring the characters created by Megan McDonald and drawn by Peter H. Reynolds to walking, talking life was the job of casting director Julie Ashton. She searched far and wide, high and low, day and night, and around the world for perfect matches!

Meet the Cast!

Illustrated Judy + Jordana Beatty = Movie Judy

Illustrated Stink + Parris Mosteller = Movie Stink

Illustrated Aunt Opal + Heather Graham = Movie Aunt Opal

Illustrated Mom + Janet Varney = Movie Mom

Illustrated Dad + Kristoffer Winters = Movie Dad

Illustrated Mr. Todd + Jaleel White = Movie Mr. Todd

Illustrated Frank Pearl + Preston Bailey = Movie Frank Pearl

Illustrated Amy Namey + Taylar Hender = Movie Amy Namey

Illustrated Rocky Zang + Garrett Ryan = Movie Rocky Zang

Illustrated Jessica Finch + Ashley Boettcher = Movie Jessica Finch

Illustrated Zeke + Jackson Odell = Movie Zeke

Illustrated Mr. Birnbaum + Robert Costanza = Movie Mr. Birnbaum

Illustrated Mrs. Birnbaum + Sharon Sachs = Movie Mrs. Birnbaum

Illustrated Mouse + Tails and Tux = Movie Mouse

A Star Is Born

The first Judy Moody book was published in April 2000. Since then, she has starred in at least twelve novels, two activity books, a journal, and now a movie! The book series has been published in more than twenty countries and languages. Ooh-la-la!

  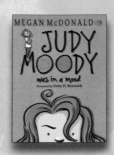

2000: first-ever cover *2005: a new look!* *2010: the 10th anniversary edition!*

Judy Moody was in a mood. Not a good mood. A bad mood.

The movie *Judy Moody and the NOT Bummer Summer* was shot in the summer and fall of 2010. It was produced by Smokewood Entertainment, and opened in theaters in 2011.

Once Upon a Time . . .

It's been called the Toilet Paper Club. It's been called the Totally Presents Club. But just what exactly *is* the T.P. Club? And how did it all start?

Once upon a time, the author of the Judy Moody books, Megan McDonald, was a kid. She had four older sisters. The sisters always had secret clubs. One time, while they were on a family vacation, the sisters caught a toad. They convinced Megan to pick it up. She held it in her hand. In no time, she felt something warm and wet. Toad pee!

So Megan McDonald became a lifetime member of the Toad Pee Club. Just like Judy Moody, Stink, and her friends Rocky and Frank. Who will become the newest member of the Toad Pee Club? Mr. Todd? Jessica Finch? You'll have to watch the movie to find out!

You, too, can become a member of the Toad Pee Club. All you have to do is pick up a toad! And wait . . . Do you feel anything? Eeeuw!

T.P. Club meeting. Be there or be a square-pants.

Nice Toady!

Judy "Scoops" Moody Talks to

JM: So, you're the producer, huh? How did you even find out about me, then get the idea to turn me, Judy Moody, into a real-live big-screen MOVIE?

SSM: *When she was in second grade, my daughter, Camryn, brought home a book about you.*

JM: Cool beans! Say more.

SSM: *We read it together and laughed our pants off. I knew then that I wanted to turn your story into a feature film.*

JM: Are you, or anybody in your family, in the movie?

SSM: *My husband, Gary, is the cabdriver when Aunt Opal arrives. My daughter, Camryn, is the zombie cheerleader who calls you "Hairhead" in the movie-theater scene. And my son, Cable, is Lobster Boy in the movie theater. You also see him pop out of the bouncy castle.*

JM: Do you have ideas about more movies you want to make?

SSM: *Oh, I have tons. I want to make a romantic comedy, an action movie, a fully animated kids' film. But first, we're going to rock the sequel to Judy Moody. High five!*

Sarah, Cable, and Gary Magness

Sarah Siegel-Magness, V.I.P. (aka Very Important Producer)

Sarah Siegel-Magness, along with her husband, Gary Magness, is the producer of *Judy Moody and the NOT Bummer Summer*, which means that the idea to turn the Judy Moody series into a movie was hers! And it means that she made it all possible. First she hired Megan McDonald and Kathy Waugh to write the screenplay. Then she hired John Schultz to direct the movie. Then she hired the bazillion other people needed to make a movie. Sarah and her husband are the founders of the production company Smokewood Entertainment.

The whole family gets in a Judy Moody mood!

Cable, Lobster Boy!

Camryn, zombie cheerleader

Sarah and Camryn at the circus.

THE MEGA-RARE NOT BUMMER SUMMER DARE IS ON!

ROAR! It's not bad enough that Mom and Dad are heading to California, leaving Judy and Stink with Aunt Awful (er, Opal), but now Judy's two best friends are going Splitsville, too. Just when it looks like her summer is going to be BOR-ing—eureka!—Judy comes up with the most thrill-a-delic plan ever. Get ready for a race involving tightrope walking, Scream Monster riding, and way more! Add in a treasure hunt for Judy's teacher, a midnight stakeout, a runaway ice-cream truck, and a dash of Bigfoot, and what have you got? Presto whammo, the Judy Moodiest summer ever!

Score your own Thrill Points!

Want to score some thrill points of your own? Look for the Thrill Points boxes or arrows as you read the book. The chart on page 144 will help you keep track!

Dare Chart designed by Brittany Macwhorter

Searching for Mr. Todd

You'll put me back together, right?

The Great Judy-a-Rini will not falllll . . . !

WHAT WAS THAT?

Watch out for dead jellyfish!

Mine!

Scream Monsterrrrr!

Did somebody say
Poop Picnic?

A Midsummer Night's Scream

After him! Go-go-
go-go-go-go!

★ ★ 21 ★ ★

Judy "Scoops" Moody Talks to

JM: So, you're gonna play me on the big screen, huh?

JB: Yep. It's very exciting! RARE!

JM: Did you have to get your hair cut to look like me?

JB: Yes. That was REALLY scary. Also sad because I've never had a haircut, really, just a trim, and I've been trying to grow it really long forever.

JM: You're from Australia! Was it hard to learn to speak with an American accent?

JB: What really helped was coming to the United States and being around American kids. I had a dialect coach, too, Francie Brown, and she really helped me at the beginning with tons of difficult words and sayings.

JM: What's your favorite thing about the United States that you don't have in Australia?

JB: I got to chew mint-chip ice-cream gum! Also, I got to go to the American Girl store, which we don't have in Australia, and I started collecting Silly Bandz. I learned about geocaching and found my first treasure box in Hollywood! And I'm hoping to taste a s'more before I leave. We don't have those in Sydney.

JM: What do you like about playing . . . ME?

JB: You have an exciting life. You're always up for some sort of adventure. You're very keen to get things done—I like that. You have so many crazy ideas and such a good imagination.

JORDANA BEATTY (aka JUDY MOODY)

JM: I hate to brush my hair. How many times a day did you have to get your hair messed up to make it look like mine?

JB: *Between every single take. That probably adds up to about a hundred times a day!*

JM: What would you like to do that would be thrill-a-delic?

JB: *Swim with dolphins! Also, I'd love to go to Washington, D.C. And I'd like to see the Statue of Liberty someday.*

JM: In real life, do you think you're like me?

JB: *I like mood rings a lot, and I love to read Nancy Drew books, and purple is my favorite color. Also, I can raise one eyebrow like you do!*

JM/JB: Same-same!

The Bride of Frankenstein goes to school with Bill Clark, studio teacher.

With her parents,
Sean and Nerida

With her movie brother,
Parris Mosteller
(aka Stink)

Jordana shows off her book autographed by Megan McDonald
AND Peter H. Reynolds! DOUBLE RARE!

Jordana Beatty, the young actress who plays Judy Moody, is an Aussie! That means she's from Australia. In order to play Judy Moody, Jordana had to learn how to speak with an American accent. The words she had the most trouble with?

- **jawbreaker** (In Australia, it's pronounced JOO-wah BRAY-kah.)
- **California**
- **idea**
- **Popsicle** (Jordana kept saying "popstickle.")
- **record**
- **Super-cali-fragi-listic-expi-thrilla-delic!**

Just as an athlete needs to warm up the body for a game or a meet, an actor or actress needs to warm up his or her mouth for a performance. Acting coaches on the set had the kids run through a bunch of tongue twisters. Here are a few they had to practice:

- Unique New York. You know you need unique New York.
- Any noise annoys an oyster, but a noisy noise annoys the oyster most.
- A box of biscuits, a box of mixed biscuits, and a biscuit mixer.

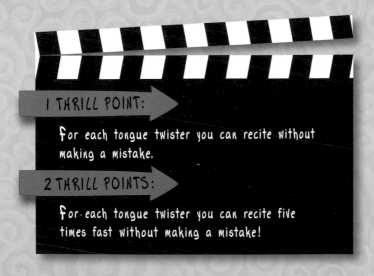

1 THRILL POINT:

For each tongue twister you can recite without making a mistake.

2 THRILL POINTS:

For each tongue twister you can recite five times fast without making a mistake!

MOODY SQUARED

Mrs. Moody is played by Janet Varney. Mr. Moody is played by Kristoffer Winters. Here's a little quiz about the actors. Can you guess—Mom or Dad?

THRILL POINT For each correct answer!

1. Which actor is a comedian?
2. Which actor has played a high-school principal?
3. Which actor grew up in New Jersey?
4. Which actor starred on a fictional TV show called *One Car, Two Car, Red Car, Blue Car*?
5. Which actor starred in *Catwoman* with Halle Berry?
6. Which actor has blond hair in real life?
7. Which actor played a character named Zilbor?
8. Which actor has three aliases spelled three different ways?

Answers on page 136

DO NOT DISTURB

Welcome to the one-and-only room of Judy Moody! Have you ever wanted to live in a mini-museum? Judy is a collector of stuff, from Band-Aids to grouchy pencils, erasers to pizza tables. Take a tour of her bedroom on the next two pages and see what collections you can spot.

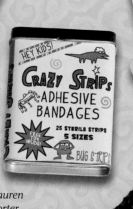

Do Not Disturb! Judy Moody is spending the Rest of the Summer in her Room!

HEY KIDS! Crazy Strips ADHESIVE BANDAGES 25 STERILE STRIPS 5 SIZES · FREE ONE INSIDE! · BUG STRIPS

These props designed by Lauren Day and Brittany Macwhorter

2 THRILL POINTS:

for each of the items you find on the next two pages:

- Class 3T photo
- Snow globe collection
- Hedda Get Betta
- Me Collage
- Giraffe Award

Hey, John and Jordana! Where's the ceiling?

Judy "Scoops" Moody Talks to

A film director keeps the "big picture" in mind while also paying attention to every detail, from costumes to makeup to props to lighting to special effects and more. He works with the writer to polish a screenplay. He directs the actors in how to play their parts and say their lines. He instructs the crew about how a scene should be set up, lit, filmed, and edited. And the list goes on. Phew!

JM: How old were you when you made your first movie?

JS: *I was twelve years old when I made* Skateboard Story, *a short film.*

JM: So you've been making movies since you were twelve. When did you know that you wanted to be a movie director?

JS: *Well, I've always been a director, starting with* Skateboard Story. *The trick was turning what I loved doing into a paying job and keeping it fun. And I totally got to do that on* Judy Moody and the NOT Bummer Summer!

JM: What other films have you directed?

JS: *There's* Aliens in the Attic, When Zachary Beaver Came to Town, *and* Like Mike, *to name a few that kids might like.*

JM: What made you want to direct a film about me?

JS: *You have a great energy and spirit that kids of any age can relate to.*

JM: What was the most fun you had while making the movie?

JOHN SCHULTZ, DIRECTOR

JS: *Surfing! Spending a day on a sunny beach teaching Preston Bailey to bodysurf and fighting those crazy waves! Also, seeing Jordana face the waves as they grew huge during her close-ups was unbelievable. She is so brave!*

JM: If a kid wants to be a movie director, what advice might you have for him or her?

JS: *Be a director now. Start making movies today. Draw each shot you will shoot, then get your hands on a camera. If you don't have a camera, put on a play with your friends.*

JM: What scene in the movie would you tell kids they absolutely, positively, for-sure can NOT miss?

JS: *I would tell them that they absolutely, positively, for-sure can NOT chicken out and close their eyes when Judy and Stink go into the woods at night to find Bigfoot!*

John checks out the camera and lighting setup for an indoor scene.

Reviewing film footage with Sarah Siegel-Magness, Megan McDonald, Richard Haynes, and Andrew Sugerman.

ZOMBIE MOVIE

"Beware of the Blob! It creeps, and leaps, and glides and slides . . ." Thrills! Chills! Blobs! Globs! In the 1950s, monster and alien movies became super popular. *Creature from the Black Lagoon* and *I Was a Teenage Frankenstein* were two blockbusters filmed in black and white when special effects were just beginning. John Schultz, the director, thought it would be fun to show a movie within a movie. So he decided to make his own black-and-white fifties-style zombie movie for Judy and Frank to watch at the Evil Creature Double Feature. All he needed was one screaming woman, a few undead zombies, and maybe, just maybe . . . a runaway eyeball!

2 THRILL POINTS:

If you watch one of John Schultz's earlier movies

4 THRILL POINTS:

If you watch two of John Schultz's earlier movies

6 THRILL POINTS:

If you watch three!

STORYBOARDS

Do you like drawing comics? Then you could be a story-board artist! The director has to plan every shot and angle in the film. A storyboard artist takes the directors' rough sketches and draws the entire movie shot by shot. A random sampling of single storyboard frames:

Full storyboard pages outlining part of a scene at the circus.

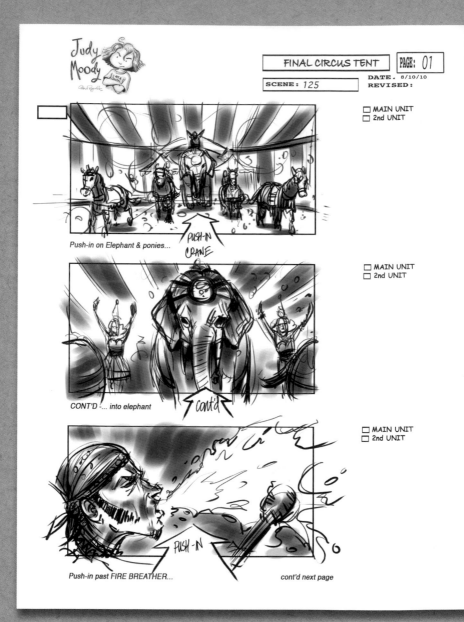

Judy Moody

☐ MAIN UNIT
☐ 2nd UNIT

OPAL, JUDY, STINK, FRANK
ZEKE, BIRNBAUMS

Cont'd - PUSH-IN to our group...

CRANE cont'd

☐ MAIN UNIT
☐ 2nd UNIT

cont'd

CONT'D -... push-in all the way to Judy

☐ MAIN UNIT
☐ 2nd UNIT

Angle on ponies / jugglers trotting past CAM

MOUSE, FELINE STARLET

The star feline on the set of *Judy Moody and the NOT Bummer Summer* is for sure and absolute positive . . . Mouse! This Moody cat has real stage presence, with an attitude certain to capture the attention of big studio executives. Mouse is waiting for her callback audition from famous director Steven Spielberg. Will she get the call?

JAWS, BOTANICAL SUPERSTAR

Jaws is Judy Moody's pet Venus flytrap. What was Jaws's favorite part of being on a movie set? Craft services, aka the food truck! Coming right up: burger (extra rare) and fresh flies—hold the ketchup!

In rehearsal

Ready and . . . action!

A flawless performance. Breathtaking!

Jaws is always on time and ready to perform.

No plants were harmed in the making of *Judy Moody and the NOT Bummer Summer*. Sadly, the same cannot be said about the flies.

HOME, SWEET HOME

117 Croaker Road
Frog Neck Lake, Virginia

Judy Moody and her family live in Virginia, the state of Pocahontas and Thomas Jefferson. Furthermore, they live in a town called Frog Neck Lake. (Oops! Sorry, Toady!)

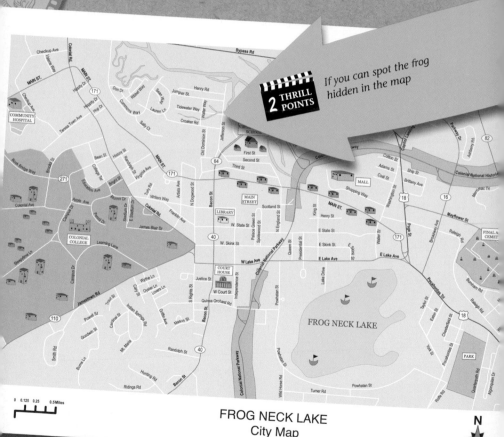

2 THRILL POINTS If you can spot the frog hidden in the map

FROG NECK LAKE
City Map

This map of Frog Neck Lake is based on a map of Williamsburg, Virginia, where Megan McDonald used to live!

★ ★ 40 ★ ★

The Moodys' movie house was in Studio City, California, more than two thousand miles away from Virginia!

Once the right house was found by the location scouts, it was painted to look spick-and-span for the movie. The house was made to look like a typical Virginia house, which meant that the front yard had to have oak trees (NOT palm trees). It also had to have enough space for a Bigfoot statue! Tons of roses in bloom added to the charm.

After

Before

Check out the pink front door! This house could win the Jessica Finch Seal of Approval.

The perfect Moody *backyard* was found in the town of South Pasadena, California—fifteen miles away from the perfect Moody *house*! It was chosen for its large, leafy trees—perfect for a backyard Bigfoot encounter!

After

Before

Aunt Opal was here!

A tree, a trap, a tent . . . and a whole lot of movie equipment and crew!

The only thing missing was the Moodys' backyard creek. Trying to find a babbling brook in Los Angeles in the summer was next to impossible. But that didn't stop the location manager, Kristi Frankenheimer. It took three days and some giant backhoes to make a realistic creek bed in the middle of the hot California desert. After the creek was filled with water, a truck-load of shrubs and trees was brought in to line the banks. *Voilà!* Instant Virginia creek.

A creek here?

Are you sure?

Presto change-o—a creek!

Watch out for toads!

WELCOME TO
FROG NECK LAKE, VIRGINIA

Judy Moody and the NOT Bummer Summer begins on the last day of school. When the final bell rings, kids pour out the door of San Rafael Elementary School, in Pasadena, California, which stood in for the Virginia Dare School.

School's out for summer! The colorful mural on the brick wall was painted just for the movie. What happened to it afterward? It stayed: a gift to SRES!

Virginia Dare School welcomes YOU!

★ ★ 44 ★ ★

The Glendora Village Pet Shop in the town of Glendora, California, was made to look like Fur & Fangs for the movie. Puppies, kittens, rabbits, guinea pigs, a parrot, and even a chinchilla became stars for a day.

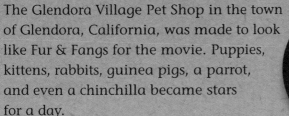

Turn to page 109. Can you spot this storefront in the background?

Stink stops in at Fur & Fangs to talk Bigfoot with Zeke.

Domenico's Jr. in Glendora was happy to pretend to be Gino's, the Moodys' favorite pizza joint. Sorry to say—they do not serve tuna-fish pizza, Stink's favorite, but they're happy to pile on the anchovies!

Waiting for the pizza

Pet store and pizza place graphics created by Teresa Keith

★ ★ 45 ★ ★

Judy and Frank try to score some thrill points on the Scream Monster roller coaster at Scare Devil Island. In fact, they are riding Goliath at Six Flags Magic Mountain in Valencia, California. This real-life rocket ship of a roller coaster will have you white-knuckling the safety bar in front of you until your hands are numb. Trust us: it's not for beginners! Built in 2000, Goliath is a steel hypercoaster that will have you hyperventilating just from looking at it. It combines a twister with an out-and-back layout. It once held world records for longest drop and top speed.

WARNING: Intense g-force may make you pull a Frank Pearl (aka upchuck!). Tip: Skip the blue cotton candy!

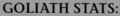

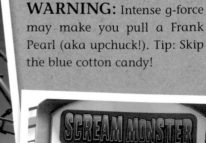

GOLIATH STATS:
- Height: 235 feet
- Angle of descent: 61°
- G-force: 4.5 g's (and we don't mean guinea pigs!)
- Drop: 255 feet
- Top speed: 85 mph

The Warner Grand Theatre is an old-fashioned movie house in San Pedro, California. It opened its doors on January 20, 1931. The owner nicknamed it the "Castle of Your Dreams," because it looks like an Art-Deco palace, complete with fancy ceilings and chandeliers. Add a host of wandering zombies, some mummies, and a mutant lobster, and it became the perfect place for Judy Moody and Frank Pearl to watch a Friday night Evil Creature Double Feature.

How do you turn a FUN Zone into an UN Zone? Knock off the letter F, of course. Find a spot by the water in San Pedro, California, and import some rusty old amusement park rides: one creaky Ferris wheel, two giant broken teacups, a few broken-down bumper cars. . . . Are we having UN-fun yet?

Painting by Cynthia Charette

It was 113 degrees the day of filming—so hot that it broke the official Los Angeles city thermometer!

IN A TIGER-STRIPES MOOD
THE WRITERS TALK WITH
MARY JANE FORT, COSTUME DESIGNER

M&R: What was your favorite costume for the character of Judy Moody?

MJF: *I would have to say the Bride of Frankenstein! (see pages 86 and 132) I asked myself, "What would Judy do?" I thought she might rummage through her clothes and find an old purple tutu, so I started there.*

M&R: How do you start designing a wardrobe for a movie character?

MJF: *First, I try to get inside the character's head by reading the books and the screenplay. Then I visit real classrooms and look at what kids that age are wearing. I scour children's books and illustrations. I spend a lot of time thinking and trying to get the colors in my mind's eye. I look at European fashion, because often their fashion trends are ahead of the United States. Then I begin to sketch. . . .*

M&R: Did you have fun designing Aunt Opal's worldly costumes?

MJF: *From the minute you meet Opal, you want to know her. Her clothes give you an immediate sense of who she is. So in the first scene with Opal, I dressed her in cutoff shorts with blue boots, a crazy fur vest, a bright shoulder bag, and lots of accessories, including her signature armful of bangles and bracelets.*

M&R: What was another fun costume to make?

MJF: *Stink's berry-bush costume.*

M&R: What was the most difficult or challenging costume you had to design?

MJF: *That would be Judy's last-day-of-school tiger-striped pajama pants. (see pages 14 and 83) None of the animal prints I found looked right, so they had to be hand-designed and made. There are so many factors that went into making those pj's—printing techniques, the weight of the fabric, color passes trying to make them look worn rather than brand-new. All in all, the design took a few months to develop.*

ALL DRESSED UP

Using the personalities and interests of each character as her guide, Mary Jane Fort built a particular look, theme, or color range around each. For Rocky, it was hints of his circus roots. For Frank, it was all about preppy and plaid (and a little nerdy). Amy Namey had flower power. Jessica Finch, of course, couldn't get enough of pink. Zeke was the safari dude, and Stink was horizontal stripes, T-shirts with words, and some serious camo. Aunt Opal was fitted out with exotic textures, luxurious fabrics, jewel colors—a dazzling wardrobe collected from all corners of the world.

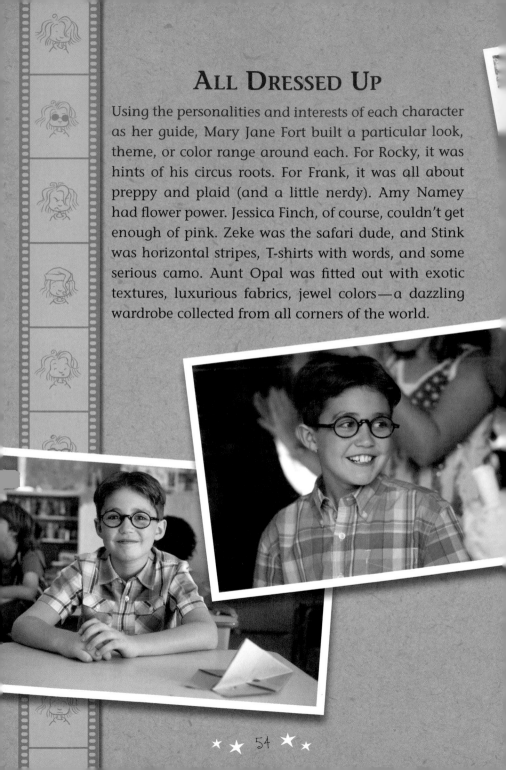

IN A BAD HAIR DAY MOOD

Costumes are step one in creating a character's look. Step two: hair and makeup. Some of the wildest dos? Judy's messy mop and moody curl, Stink's serious spikes, Zeke's parroty streaks, Mom's flippy wig, and Aunt Opal's wavy locks.

Wigged Out!

The kids on the set loved giving nicknames to everything, even the hairpieces!

- Janet's wig: Lynn Masters (after a famous Hollywood hairstylist)
- Heather's wigs: Nathalie and Natasha
- Heather's hair extensions: Nikita
- Taylar's hair extensions: Nana
- Jordana's Bride of Frankenstein wigs: Nancy and Nina
- Jordana's hairbrush: Nikki (Garrett wanted to name it Goblin.)

The curls attached to Jordana's hair each had a particular mood and personality, according to hairstylist Ramona Fleetwood. Jordana named them, of course: Ramona, Bobbi Sue, Nona, Hero Opal, and Navangelina for the blue-puke curl.

3 THRILL POINTS:

If you go to the movie *Judy Moody and the NOT Bummer Summer* dressed as Judy, Stink, Frank, Rocky, Amy, Jessica, Zeke, or Jessica Finch

+5 THRILL POINTS:

If you get your friends to do the same

JUDY "SCOOPS" MOODY TALKS TO

JM: Stink's favorite food is silver-dollar pancakes. What is your favorite?

PM: *My favorite food is steamed clams. Yum! I could eat them all day and night.*

JM: How old are you?

PM: *I'm eight.*

JM: Stink likes to read the *S* encyclopedia. How about you?

PM: *I read the Pokémon encyclopedia, but mostly I like inventing stuff. Like on set, the chairs don't have built-in tables. I want to invent the table chair. Another one is the Fan Shirt 3000. That's because it is so-o-o-o, so hot on set sometimes. I also invented a dice game about the Moodys. Especially Stink. It's called Scatters. It even has kitty litter in it!*

JM: Say no more. What do you like to do when you are not on set?

PM: *Swim. Especially in the ocean. I sometimes swim for a whole hour. A lot of days I swim for two miles.*

JM: Do you have any brothers or sisters?

PM: *In fact, I have four brothers. One older, three younger. NO sisters allowed!*

JM: How many pieces of hot dog did you have to eat or put in your mouth for the backyard fondue scene?

PM: *Gag me. You had to ask. It was over fifty. Oogley-boogley!*

PARRIS MOSTELLER (aka STINK)

In one shot, I have to spit out a hot-dog chunk. I spat it out and it landed on my arm and stuck there and we all cracked up. The director had to yell "Cut," he was laughing so hard.

JM: Did you ever enter your shoes in a smelly sneaker contest?

PM: *No, but I invented smell cups on set and sold them for a dollar each. There were all kinds of smells. Flowers. Tree bark. Dirt. Mint. Rose petals.*

JM: Sweet!

STINK'S FILM-O-PEDIA

Stink is a fact freak. He's also gaga over gadgets. So a movie set is like a dream come true for him. Here are just a few of the tid-bits Stink, the human encyclopedia, picked up in Hollywood. Lights, camera, *fact*-ion!

"And CUT!": What the director calls out to end the filming of a scene; sound and film stop rolling.

"Background": The verbal signal to extras in a scene—such as a dog walker, a jogger, a shopper—to begin moving. This kind of detail makes the movie feel as if it could be taking place in real life.

Three extras stroll through a park. The one in the middle is the movie director's wife, Esther—for real!

Boom: A long pole used to hold a microphone over the heads of the actors so that it won't show up on film. (The most common mistake in a movie is being able to spot a boom or its shadow in a scene!)

Randy Johnson, boom operator, is dressed for a wet day at the office!

Checking the gate: If you spot someone peering into the wrong end of a camera lens, chances are he's "checking the gate:" making sure that no hair, lint, or other gunk has snuck inside. One always checks the gate before moving on to film a new scene. If the gate is dirty, the scene will need to be reshot.

Cherry picker: A crane that can hold a camera, a diffuser, a microphone, or other piece of equipment high and out of sight. Chances are you've seen telephone or electric workers use cherry pickers, too.

This cherry picker is holding a diffuser over the Moodys' backyard.

Lightbanks: An array of tools used to create and control light. They are often soft white boxes, called Chimeras, fitted over lights.

Clapboard: Also called the clapsticks or clapper, it contains information for each shot in a movie: title, director, scene number, date, time, etc. The clapping noise it makes is later used by editors to match up the sound with the picture.

Diffuser: Diffusers look a bit like big white sheets or canvasses, and are used to tone down sunlight or other bright lights. They come in different sizes and types.

Jim Leidholdt pushes the camera along the dolly tracks.

Dolly: A dolly is NOT a toy baby. It's a platform on wheels to which the camera can be attached. It's great for filming someone on the move, maybe riding a bike or running after Bigfoot!

End crawl: You know that long list of names in tiny type that comes at the end of a movie? That's called the end crawl.

Extras: Also called "background artists" or "background performers," extras are actors hired when a scene calls for large numbers or crowds of people. They don't usually have speaking lines.

Focus puller: Usually the first camera assistant (also known as the 1AC, and the person who heads up the camera department). Pulling focus means to measure the distance from the back of the camera lens to the subject being filmed. This measurement is used to get the camera focus just right.

Jorge Sanchez, 1AC, has his tape measure in hand, ready to pull focus.

Gaffer: The gaffer is the director of photography's right-hand person and is in charge of all lighting throughout the movie, indoors and out.

Grip: The job of the grip department is to cut, shape, and manipulate all light sources—electric or natural—based on the gaffer's instructions.

Balloon lights are used to lend a moonlit glow to a nighttime scene.

"It's a wrap!": That's what the director says when the last shot of the day has been completed and he or she is ready to go home and have dinner.

Magazine: A container loaded with film and attached to the movie camera. Usually very visible, as here with its red stripe.

"Picture's up!": This is what the production assistant announces to let everyone know that the cameras will soon be rolling. *Quiet down! Places, everyone!*

Director of photography Shawn Maurer's camera is fully loaded and ready to roll.

Process trailer: Cameras, sound equipment, producers, the script supervisor, and the director are piled onto this mini studio-on-wheels for shooting scenes on the go.

"Ready and . . . action!": When the director calls for "action," the actors start saying their lines and, well, acting!

This process trailer is towing Humphrey, the Moody car, so that the camera can shoot straight into the car through the windshield.

Randall Stone, 2AC, lays down some stand Ts.

"Roll sound": The order to begin recording sound on the set.

Stand Ts: Colored markers on the ground that tell an actor or actress exactly where to stand for a scene. All actors and actresses are marked at all times with their own color, and the job of marking falls to the second camera assistant (2AC).

Steadicam: A camera that is worn by the camera operator with the help of a mechanical harness. The whole thing, often referred to as a rig, can weigh forty-five to fifty-five pounds! As the name suggests, it cuts down the amount of wobble or shake created by the camera operator's movements.

Jody Miller is both the steadicam operator and the A-Camera Operator.

"Take 1, 2, 3 . . .": At the click of the clap-board, cameras are set to roll. The number of takes on the clapboard indicates how many times a scene has been filmed.

Video Village: Video Village is where the producers, director, script supervisors, writers, and other crew gather to sit and watch the video monitors, which show the shot being filmed at that moment.

Walk and talk: Just what it sounds like! A scene in which the actors are being filmed as they are walking and talking. A steadicam or a camera mounted to a dolly might be used in a walk and talk.

The zeppelin was used during the crazy bicycle ride. Also pictured is a process trailer for camera and crew and a small process trailer for bike and riders!

Zeppelin: Looking a lot like a feather duster, a zeppelin is attached to a microphone to reduce the sound of air or wind. Great for action scenes in which the camera is moving at high speeds.

And that's a wrap!

Shawn Maurer preparing the camera for a scene featuring Janet Varney

Shawn Maurer with executive producer Andrew Sugerman

Shawn Maurer, DP

The director of photography (DP), or cinematographer, is the crew member who works most closely with the director during a film shoot. The director has the vision for how a scene should look, and it's up to the DP to pull together and manage the tools—cameras, lenses, filters, film stock, lighting—that will visually capture and then record that vision. This places the DP in charge of all camera operators, camera assistants, focus pullers, and lighting crews. It takes a lot of hard work, attention to detail, and experience to become a DP.

Judy "Scoops" Moody Talks to

If you've ever seen the TV show *Family Matters*, you may recognize "Mr. Todd" early in his acting career, at the age of twelve. Jaleel White, the actor who played Urkel on that show, is all grown up now. Judy Moody caught up with him on the set of *Judy Moody and the NOT Bummer Summer*.

JM: Mr. Todd is the World's Greatest Teacher. Who was *your* greatest teacher?

JW: *There were so many! I went to nine different schools throughout elementary and middle school.*

JM: If you had to pick just one, who would it be?

JW: *How about two? I have to credit Miss Thor, my seventh-grade English teacher, with teaching me how to construct sentences. But in fourth grade, I had the best teacher, Ms. McDonald. I was teacher's pet! I got straight A's that year, except for one U.*

JM: No way! U is for Unsatisfactory! Stink got one of those in gym. What subject did you get a U in?

JW: *Conduct!*

JM: What's conduct?

JALEEL WHITE (aka MR. TODD)

JW: *Conduct is how you behave in school. You get a U in it when you've been goofing off instead of studying!*

JM: Sweet! If you were in my class, you'd have to go to Antarctica to "chill out."

JW: *Don't forget: I am Mr. Todd. I invented Antarctica.*

"WHAT I DID ON MY SUMMER VACATION"
by Mr. Todd

Have you ever wondered where your teachers go when the final bell rings on the last day of school? Well, it might surprise you to find out that we *don't* hang out in our classrooms all summer.

We catch up on hobbies
I grow a mean tomato, I love reading mysteries, and I like to hike. A friend of mine likes skydiving and bungee jumping!

We take classes
Some teachers take classes to learn about new subjects. That's right: when you're not in class, your teacher just might be. I'm thinking I'd like to learn how to play the didgeridoo. And I should brush up on my Italian before I take another trip to Bologna! There's always snake charming, too.

We travel
Teachers need vacations, too. A few of the places I'd like to visit: Patagonia, Australia, New Zealand, Antarctica, Mars.

We sleep in
Teachers like sleeping in on summer mornings almost as much as you do!

We get a summer job
One summer I worked at the Pickle Barrel deli making sandwiches. Another summer, I had a really *cool* job! (Hint: Watch the movie to find out what it was!) Maybe your teacher has a surprising summer job, too! Counting cheetahs in Africa?

Repairing coral reefs in the Bahamas? Brushing manatee teeth in Sarasota, Florida? Some other summer jobs teachers have held:

- waiter
- fishing guide
- professional singer
- soccer camp coach
- tour guide
- yoga instructor
- bookseller
- Segway rider
- yacht chef
- emergency medical technician
- dog walker
- house painter
- card dealer
- lifeguard

Look for *your* teacher at the mall, the park, the pool, or the public library.

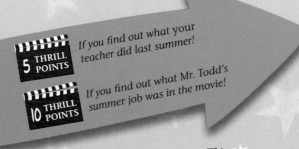

5 THRILL POINTS If you find out what your teacher did last summer!

10 THRILL POINTS If you find out what Mr. Todd's summer job was in the movie!

JUDY "SCOOPS" MOODY TALKS TO

JM: Did you have to do anything special to prepare for the role of Rocky?

GR: *When I found out my character goes to circus camp, I went online and learned how to juggle.*

JM: What's your favorite magic trick?

GR: *The levitating salt trick. You pour a bunch of salt on the table. Then you balance the saltshaker on one edge, and it looks like it's floating.*

JM: What is your favorite scene in the movie?

GR: *The big good-bye scene at Rocky's house, because it's all about me—ha, ha! I got tossed upside down into Gilbert Grape (the car I drive off in with my mom).*

JM: Was it slimy to have to pick up a real toad in the creek?

GR: *Are you kidding? It was great! Toads are fun. There were actually three toads—a small, a medium, and a large—and they were all kind of squishy.*

JM: What do you like to do when you are not acting?

GR: *I love to read. Right now I'm reading* The Mysterious Benedict Society, *and it's awesome!*

JM: How old are you?

GR: *Eleven.*

GARRETT RYAN (aka ROCKY ZANG)

JM: Do you have any brothers or sisters?

GR: *Nope. I'm an only, so I'm in the Only Club with Ashley and Jordana. But I think it would be super-cool to have a big crazy family like Rocky's circus family.*

The Zang Family Circus

THE DAZZLING
WHIZ-BANG ZANGS PRESENT
A CAVALCADE OF DELIGHTS AND
DERRING-DO,
WHICH IS TO SAY,

AN ASTONISHING AND ENTIRELY SATISFYING ARRAY OF
MUSICAL, COMEDIC, ZOOLOGICAL, AND ACROBATIC
ENTERTAINMENT FOR LADIES, GENTLEMEN, YOUNG MISSES,
YOUNG MASTERS, AND EVEN THE LITTLE *BAMBINI*.

20 THRILL POINTS   If you put on your own backyard circus

That's a real elephant in the circus scene. But did Rocky really have to scoop the poop? Not exactly. The props department made balls of fake elephant poo, but they ran into a major pooper blooper! The poo was made of silicon (like rubber), so it bounced! They had to go back to the drawing board. It took four or five false starts, but finally . . . . *PLOPPPP!* No more poppy, peppy poop!

IN A SAME-SAME MOOD

On a movie set, stand-ins hold the place of actors while cameras and lighting are set up for a scene. A stand-in often has the same hair color, skin tone, and body type as his or her actor so that the lighting crew can get the lights just right. Stand-ins never appear on screen, but they are very important for a smooth film shoot.

Kimberly Throckmorten, stand-in for Judy, and Carla Watts, stand-in for Aunt Opal

By law, child actors are permitted to work for only a limited number of hours per day. Between takes, they study with their studio teachers. In the meantime, grown-ups who are about the same height as the kids stand in for them.

Kimberly Throckmorten and Tracey Thompson, stand-in for Stink

Kimberly Throckmorten and Frank Gieb, stand-in for Frank Pearl

Judy Moody has a famous elbow. Kasey Maline has a famous hand! Kasey was the photo double for Jordana. You might see her hand typing an e-mail or writing on the Thrill Points Chart.

Judy "Scoops" Moody Talks to

JM: What other movies have you been in, Taylar?

TH: *I just finished a movie called* Den Brother, *in which I play a girl named Abigail. It was fun because there were lots of kids and we filmed in Utah, where we got to experience snow. Not the snowman kind, the snowball kind.*

JM: Are you looking forward to being a member of the Toad Pee Club?

TH: *Ooh, ick! I have to let a real toad pee real pee on me! That is worth zero thrill points. But at least I get to wipe it off on you afterward. Hee, hee! Actually, that's my favorite scene in the movie.*

JM: Have you ever been to Borneo for real?

TH: *No. So far I've never left the United States. But someday I hope to go to Paris, France. I'm learning how to speak French right now. Ooh-la-la!*

JM: What do you like to do when you're not acting?

TH: *I'm on a dive team. And I love gymnastics and dance. Oh, and reading. Also, I love to cook. I like all the contraptions like cookie cutters, and I want to learn how to make croissants.*

JM: What's your favorite food?

TH: *Chicken and pasta.*

JM: What's your favorite pizza topping?

TH: *Does cheese count?*

TAYLAR HENDER (aka AMY NAMEY)

JM: What's your favorite color?

TH: *Pink and orange. I've always loved pink my whole life, but now orange is the new pink.*

JM: How are you like Amy Namey, the character you play?

TH: *I'm super organized. You should see Amy's suitcase! There are supposed to be ten Nancy Drew mysteries that she takes to Borneo, but there were only nine. (I counted.) By the way, I love Nancy Drew, too!*

JM: Same-same! If you were in charge of the Judy Moody movie sequel, what would it be about?

TH: *We would all go to Hawaii and swim with dolphins and ride a giant waterslide! No sharks allowed!*

JM: Rare!

AMY NAMEY'S VIDEO DIARY

Dear Judy Most Moody,

Borneo is coolness! Never in a million years would you believe all the cool stuff here. I swam with (whale) sharks and fed a baby orangutan named Peaches. I'm having a swingin' good time. (Ha, ha, ha.)

W Y W H (Wish You Were Here)

Ames

Peaches, banana, and me

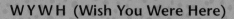

2 THRILL POINTS If you can find Borneo on a map of the world

How many thrill points is this worth?

Zip, zip, hooray!

Just hanging around

The Real Lost Tribe of Borneo
by Dr. E. Namey, PhD

The Penan people, sometimes referred to as a "lost tribe," are hunter-gatherers living in the rain forests of interior Borneo. They are noted for practicing *molong,* which means never taking more from their environment than necessary. The Penan are a generous, egalitarian people. Helping one another and working cooperatively is assumed, so much so that they have no word for *thank you* in their language. They don't need one. Logging and deforestation are now threatening the Penan way of life. Efforts are under way to block further destruction of their homeland.

JUDY "SCOOPS" MOODY TALKS TO

JM: Preston, how did you get into acting?

PB: *It was because my older brother, Brennan, is an actor. When I saw what he was doing, I realized that I wanted to do that, too. So I gave it a try.*

JM: Did you like dressing up as Frankenstein?

PB: *Totally! But trust me: it is not easy to walk or run down stairs in giant elevator shoes.*

JM: Do you have any ideas for a Judy Moody movie sequel?

PB: *I have two ideas. The first one would be that Judy, Frank, Rocky, and Amy build a time machine and then travel back or forward in time together. The second is that they would build a boat and then get stranded on an island with only a blanket to keep them warm.*

JM: How many times did you have to eat the T.P. Club meeting note in the school scene?

PB: *Seven, at least. And it didn't taste good. Bluck! It's like eating a pen or pencil.*

JM: What is your favorite scene in the movie?

PB: *Actually, there are two. I really like the theater scene with the zombies. And I like surfing in the beach scene just as much.*

JM: What do you like most about playing Frank "Eats Paste" Pearl?

PRESTON BAILEY (aka FRANK PEARL)

PB: *I like the fact that I finally get to be in a movie that's for kids. See, in the other shows or movies I've been in, I play a kid but the movie is for grown-ups.*

JM: What is your favorite pizza topping?

PB: *Cheese is my favorite. But guess what? Once I had a pizza when I was on a movie set in Hungary and it had corn and steak for toppings.*

"HOW TO RIDE A ROLLER COASTER WITHOUT SPEWING"

by Frank Pearl

1. **SIT TOWARD THE FRONT.** The farther back you sit, the faster you—and your stomach—drop after a steep climb!

2. **ON A CORKSCREW COASTER, SIT TOWARD THE BACK** so you can see what's coming. (If the people in front of you live through the turn, chances are, you will, too).

3. **DON'T RIDE RIGHT AFTER PIGGING OUT.** (Or at least eat foods that won't turn your friends blue when you throw up on them.)

4. **TRY NOT TO IMAGINE FALLING OUT OF YOUR SEAT AND GOING SPLAT,** like an overripe melon, on the ground below. Roller coasters are safety-inspected every single day.

5. **DON'T THINK ABOUT YOUR TENDER AGE,** much too young to die. Only ride if you meet the age and height rules posted.

6. **SCREAM.** A lot if you need to. Really—it helps!

Judy Moody Gets the Blues!

Click-click-click-click-click. How would you like to be ascending a 235-foot, straight-up steep hill, trying to remember your lines, thinking about your facial expressions, keeping your eyes open the whole time, with three cameras only inches from your face, and know that any second you are going to be covered in flying blue puke? That's what Jordana Beatty, aka Judy Moody, had to do in the roller-coaster scene. No, that's not a stunt double! What was the blue puke made of? Vanilla pudding! Add a blueberry granola bar, oatmeal, Rice Krispies, blue Jell-O, and—*voilà!*—Puke Monster!

2 THRILL POINTS If you've ridden a roller coaster at least once in your life

5 THRILL POINTS If you've ridden a corkscrew roller coaster with your eyes open!

Megan McDonald checks Jordana's reaction to watching herself turn blue on the roller coaster!

ARE YOU A FUN SPONGE?

"You're nothing but one big wet . . . . FUN SPONGE!"

A fun sponge is someone who's in a bad mood and sucks the fun out of everything. Take this quiz and find out where you rate on the Sponge-O-Meter.

WOULD YOU RATHER:
A. Go to circus camp?
B. Take a trip to Borneo?
C. Take your stuffed animals to obedience school?

WOULD YOU RATHER:
A. Sit through a whole entire scary movie?
B. Ride a roller coaster all day?
C. Count socks in a drawer?

WOULD YOU RATHER:
A. Make a giant hat out of a garbage-can lid?
B. Make a thrill-o-delic Thrill Points Chart?
C. Rake leaves all day without jumping in the pile?

WOULD YOU RATHER:
A. Go on a midnight stakeout?
B. Make up secret code words for your walkie-talkies?
C. Not share your night-vision goggles with anyone?

WOULD YOU RATHER:
A. Learn to walk on a tightrope?
B. Walk to Fur & Fangs?
C. Not walk to meet your friend for ice cream at Screamin' Mimi's?

WOULD YOU RATHER:
A. Catch a South American marine toad?
B. Catch a super-fast fly ball?
C. Catch a cold and stay in bed all day?

WOULD YOU RATHER:
A. Teach your cat to make toast?
B. Teach your guinea pig to do yoga?
C. Babysit a pet rock?

THRILL POINTS

Turn to page 136 to earn thrill points and find out if you're a fun sponge!

Judy "Scoops" Moody Talks to

JM: How long have you been an actress?

HG: *I've been acting since I was a teenager. Some of my first movie roles were in* Drugstore Cowboy *and* License to Drive.

JM: That's so funny that your first movie was about a kid who flunked his driving test and can't really drive. And now you have to play my aunt, who is a terrible driver!

HG: *I know!*

JM: Where did you grow up?

HG: *I grew up in Virginia.*

JM: Same-same!

HG: *My dad was in the FBI (top secret!), and my mom was a teacher. She also wrote children's books.*

JM: Cool beans! What stuff did you like to do when you were my age?

HG: *I'm a reader, and I was* way *into* Pippi Longstocking. *I love how she has special powers.*

JM: I know. She has super-human strength! I wish I could lift a horse one-handed.

HG: *I know, right?*

JM: What do you like to do when you're not acting?

HG: *I am way into yoga.*

Heather Graham (aka Aunt Opal)

JM: Hold the phone! I like yoga-not-yogurt, too. I even taught Mouse the cat some yoga poses.

HG: *I think we're a lot alike. I also like dance, cooking and eating with friends, swimming in the ocean, and scuba diving.*

JM: I heard it was your idea to do the freeze dance in the movie. That is so way cool.

HG: *And thrill-a-delic.*

JM: You seem to love music. What are you listening to right now?

HG: *Radiohead, lots of world and alternative music. I like to choose a song before my scene that helps me get into character and fits with the tone and mood of the scene.*

JM: What are you listening to today?

HG: *I've been listening to "Free" a lot, by Ultra Nate.*

JM: What did you like about the character of Aunt Opal that made you want to take the role?

HG: *I love Opal's backstory—I find the character of Aunt Opal so interesting; that she's been to art school in Berlin and traveled the world doing guerrilla art. She gets to burst onto the Moody scene, making an immediate connection with Judy and Stink, and it's just so sweet and funny and magical, like a contemporary Mary Poppins.*

In an Opalizing Mood

Judy Moody's Aunt Awful arrives with not just another suitcase—but a super-duper gigantic trunk! Inside is a traveling art studio full of paints and brushes and ribbons and stickers and beads and . . . tons more stuff for making art.

After much searching, the perfect trunk for Aunt Opal was found. It's an old, antique trunk from the Metropolitan Opera House, in New York City. One look and you just know this trunk has a history. Valerie Green, art director, spent *hours* getting the trunk gorgeously outfitted for the movie.

It belonged to a famous opera singer named Dorothy Kirsten. Kirsten, a soprano, got her start at the Metropolitan Opera singing in the role of Mimi in *La Bohème,* in 1945, and sang at the Met for the next thirty years, becoming famous for roles in *Tosca* and *Madame Butterfly.* She also starred in movies and has a star on the Hollywood Walk of Fame.

Aunt Opal's trunk of wonders

Aunt Opal is a guerrilla-not-gorilla artist. That means she makes art out of everything and puts it everywhere.

Beauty creates the Beast

Judy tries her hand at guerrilla art, too.

Garbage-can lids never looked so good!

Art, anyone?

Magical!

Set dressers make messes look great!

MOVIE MAGIC

It took a lot of artists and designers to create Judy Moody's world. From backyard to bunk bed, from park to pier, from Scream Monster to Scream Fest, it all began with reading the books and poring over the drawings. After reading the script many times over, the production designer, Cynthia Charette, began to see the geography of Judy Moody's world in her mind's eye.

With leaps of imagination, not to mention heaps of color, fabric, wallpaper, paint, artists, and craftspeople, and countless meetings and discussions with Valerie Green, art director; Don Diers, set decorator; and Mary Jane Fort, costume designer, Judy's world sprang to life.

Cynthia Charette, production designer, and Don Diers, set decorator

"The Cave": Meeting place for the
Bigfoot Believer's Association

Inside the T.P. Club tent

Amy Namey's room

A moonlit midnight stakeout

Stink's room, complete with car bed and "Stink 3000" wallpaper!

The Moodys' stairwell, a gallery that includes real baby pictures of Jordana and Parris

The Moodys' kitchen is sunny, warm, and welcoming.

The wallpaper in Judy's room was custom-made to echo the curl on the top of her head. But that's not the only place Cynthia Charette used the swirly curl shape to decorate something! She used it 61 times!

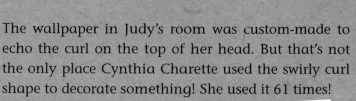

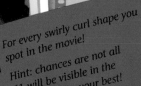

THRILL POINT For every swirly curl shape you spot in the movie!

Hint: chances are not all 61 will be visible in the final film. Do your best!

Cynthia Charette and Darwin Browne, key grip

The property master's job is to find or make any objects needed in the film. In this case, Tom Cahill had to supervise the making of a giant jellyfish, poop, and puke, among other things.

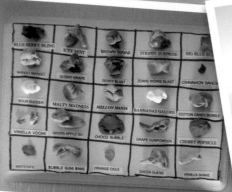

Judy's ABC gum collection

Tom Cahill displays some of his team's handiwork.

Dozens of Thrill Point charts were made for the movie.

Check out that tiger-striped seat!

The poop in the sandwiches Judy, Stink, and Aunt Opal take on their picnic was made of chocolate fondant with cranberries and rasperries. It may LOOK like scat, but it tasted like a candy bar. Yummmm!

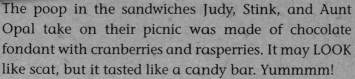

Kenneth Garrett sculpted this elephant head. Watch out below!

Bench by Aunt Opal (but not really)! Chuck Coffman was master installer and artist on this masterpiece.

Between the art, design, property, and construction teams, there were more than forty people involved in the creation of the places and things seen in *Judy Moody and the NOT Bummer Summer*.

THE BIGFOOT STATUE

A Styrofoam block, old rugs, Spanish moss, palm fronds, duct tape, tree bark . . . add some baseball eyes and *voilà!* Bigfoot lives! Fifty cents a touch!

Bigfoot by Kenneth Garrett, sculptor, and Chuck Coffman, key fabricator

Judy "Scoops" Moody Talks to

JM: What was the best part about playing Zeke? Was it that my little "bother," Stink, really looked up to you and thought you were way cool?

JO: I just love playing a character who's the opposite of me, I mean, this guy is so totally into Bigfoot, it's crazy. Also, the hairspray.

JM: Is it true that you are a brainiac? Stink says you are trying to join some super-genius Einstein club named Mental or something?

JO: It's called Mensa. You have to have a super-high IQ, and I'm off by only three points. So if you have any tips on how to get smarter fast, let me know. I'm thinking about that sleeping-on-the-dictionary thing that worked for you—when all those big vocabulary words went into your brain.

JM: Speaking of being a genius, do you go to regular school and have a teacher like Mr. Todd? What kind of things do you like to study?

JO: I'm home-schooled, so my teacher is pretty much my mom. Right now, I'm interested in astrophysics, so I read up on that a lot in my spare time.

JM: At the opening cast party, I heard you singing. Is that something you do a lot of when you are not acting? Maybe you and I should sing "On Top of Spaghetti" to drive Stink crazy!

JACKSON ODELL (aka ZEKE)

JO: *I am way into music. I play piano, drums, bass, and guitar. I sang in a choir when I was your age. I got into music from my older brother—I have 11,000 songs on my computer: John Mayer, Eric Clapton, Led Zeppelin, Jimi Hendrix, B.B. King.*

JM: Did you grow up in Hollywood, or can you tell your fans where you're from?

JO: *I'm from Colorado, but I hang out in Los Angeles a lot when I'm filming a TV show or movie. You might have seen me on an episode of* Modern Family.

JM: Are you even old enough to drive a Vespa?

JO: *I'm only thirteen, so I don't have a driver's license for real. But in the movie I do!*

No Animals Were Harmed in the Making of this Film.

Have you ever wondered where that phrase comes from? The Film & TV Unit of the American Humane Association, which monitors animal treatment on more than one thousand productions every year, makes sure that animals used in movies and on TV are happy and healthy on set. They make sure that any animal actors don't work too many hours, have good and comfortable places to live, interact well with their human and animal costars, and even if and how they can wear costumes.

The blue and yellow macaw at Fur & Fangs is a parrot named Rainbow. Macaws make great pets because of their beauty and their ability to talk. They eat seeds, nuts, fruits and vegetables, and especially enjoy pasta! *Spaghetti, anyone?*

The movie star Mouse is played by two honest-to-meow Hollywood working cats. Their names are Tux and Tails. No lie. According to Shawn Weber and Sheri Aparicio, the animal trainers and handlers, Tux is the stunt cat, and Tails is the true actor. You decide if you can spot the difference. *High five, Mouse!*

Three toads—Freddy, Ernest, and Hemingway—were used in the movie. All three are South American marine toads, also known as cane toads or giant toads. In Belize, they're even called spring chickens! *Croak, croak, cluck!*

Nugget is the name of the opossum that appears in the nighttime stakeout scene. Nugget may be afraid of Bigfoot, because she did not want to come out and swing from a tree that night. Can you blame her? Scarrryyyy!

Five talented dogs were rescued from an animal shelter: Jessie, Zoe, Bobby, Harlan, and Austin. After lots of training, these are the doggies you'll see chasing Bigfoot down Croaker Road (Judy Moody's street).

Those talented ponies at the circus are no robots! They are the very real Silver, Sassy, Charlie, and Rocky (Hey, same-same!).

Susie is a very sweet, very big twenty-five-year-old African elephant.

HONK IF YOU'RE MOODY

What does YOUR race-car bed say? Make a statement with bumper stickers.

Stink's got them on his bed. Zeke sports them on his Vespa. And the Birnbaums can be quoted: "Say it with a slogan."

got bigfoot?

Bumper stickers created by Teresa Keith and Lauren Day

If you make your own Bigfoot bumper sticker

2 THRILL POINTS

Life is Short:
Believe in Bigfoot

I BRAKE FOR... BIGFOOT

Take a Peek at Zeke's Vespa

When Zeke has to get somewhere fast, like to Fur & Fangs or a Bigfoot Believers meeting, what better way to travel than on his sleek, shiny black Vespa? Keep a sharp eye out in the movie for someone else who might take a late-night ride on this dash-about-town scooter. If you think it's Bigfoot—think again!

"Good luck, little dude. You, too, Moody Girl. Call me if you see anything. Day or night."

So You Want to Catch Bigfoot?

Camouflage netting, night-vision goggles, camcorder, whistles, coffee (blech!). Everything you need for a Bigfoot emergency. Need backup? The Birnbaums' van is at your service.

The Birnbaums' van was fitted out by Chuck Coffman, key fabricator.

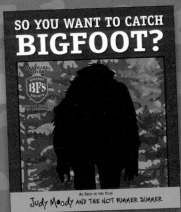

SO YOU WANT TO CATCH **BIGFOOT?**

Any Bigfooter worth his salt should read Dr. Morgan Jackson's book, *So You Want to Catch Bigfoot?* He gives lots of good tips and advice, and the Birnbaums own multiple copies. Here's just a sample from this essential volume:

THE STAKEOUT: PACK YOUR BAGS

Poor preparation could lead to a hair-raising situation. First gather the necessary supplies and Bigfoot-catching equipment. Triple-check to make sure you didn't forget anything.

Things You'll Need:

- Camouflage netting
- Night-vision goggles
- Tent
- Sleeping bag
- Binoculars
- Emergency sirens
- Whistles
- Nose clip (a Bigfoot's smell has caused some to pass out.)
- Camcorder with night vision
- TWO cameras with night vision (an extra for backup)
- Tape recorders
- Tape of vocalizations (optional)
- Supplies for building a trap
- Supplies for gathering evidence: latex gloves, tongs, tweezers, plastic bag, marker for labeling specimens
- TWO coolers—one for food and one for scat (Careful not to mix these up!)
- Journal for recording data
- Equipment for making casts of footprints
- Tranquilizer gun
- Flashlight
- Protective metallic suit
- Disguise and/or camouflage gear
- Meals, eating utensils, a thermos, and lots of coffee or hot chocolate
- *So You Want to Catch Bigfoot?* (the book!)

5 THRILL POINTS *If you read So You Want to Catch Bigfoot?*

THE PEANUT-BUTTER TRAP

Bigfoot is nuts about peanut butter, making this a trap it can't resist. How it works in a nutshell: A net is hung from a tree. Peanut-butter jars are attached to the net. When Bigfoot yanks on a jar, the net falls on it, and—wham!—you've snagged your first Sasquatch.

WHAT YOU'LL NEED:

- 30 jars of peanut butter
- 30 pieces of string (3 feet each)
- Net or hammock
- Old hooded sweatshirt (large)
- Old baseball cap
- Glue
- Leaves
- Twigs
- Berries (Any berries will do.)

Total camo!

1. Create a berry-bush disguise. Glue leaves, twigs, and berries onto the sweatshirt and cap. Set aside.

2. Hang a large net from various branches of a tree. Make sure the netting is hidden among the leaves and not in sight.

3. Tie thirty peanut-butter jars to the netting. They should dangle low enough for Bigfoot to see and reach.

4. Put on your disguise.

5. Hide and wait.

LETTING BIGFOOT GO

Untie several jars of peanut butter from the net and quickly roll them over to Bigfoot. While it's distracted by the peanut butter, slowly begin pulling the net off and throw more jars as far as you can into the woods. Bigfoot will chase the jars, not you.

Flashlight? Check. Camouflage netting? Check. Night-vision goggles? Check. Walkie-talkies? Check. No sleeping, no snoring. Check. And now the wait. What was that? Stink? Did you hear that? Do you think it's—

CODE RED! CODE RED! BIGGGGGFOOOOOTTTTT!

The trap has been set!

20 THRILL POINTS For having your own Bigfoot stakeout!

The Bigfoot stakeout has officially begun.

Judy and Stink tiptoed farther and farther into the gloom.

"Holy macaroni! It's . . . it's him!"

ICE CREAM AND BAND-AIDS

As a child, Megan McDonald grabbed a dime, ran down the street, and chased after the ice-cream truck nearly every day of summer. One day, it took forever to find a dime, so she had to run up a steep hill to try to catch the truck on the next street. *Crash! Bang! OOPS!* She fell down the hill and had to get twelve stitches. Ouch! That's one big Band-Aid and no ice cream. Her experience inspired the ice-cream truck chase in *Judy Moody and the NOT Bummer Summer*.

HOLD FOR FILE

Benjamin Moore Colors

2078-30
Royal Fuscia

2079-40
Springtime Bloom

OC-122
Cotton Balls

2060-30
Seaport Blue

OC-66
Snow White

Turn to page 34 for a look at the real truck.

IN A FAKE-O BRAND MOOD

While the town of Frog Neck Lake is based, loosely, on Williamsburg, Virginia, it is not an actual place you can find on any real map. To give it a sense of being real-but-not-real, just about everything was made up and given a name by Megan McDonald herself, including products, places, street names, bumper stickers, and labels.

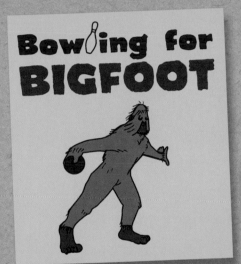

Bobbi Sue's PUPPY CHOW

"Because your puppy deserves the best."

Can you figure out which movie VIP this chow is named for?

This brand name came from a Peter H. Reynolds illustration in Judy Moody Saves the World!

CONk Peanut Butter

257

TAXI | SHIFT 2 GREEN
—FROG NECK LAKE, VA—

ADOPT A HERMIT CRAB!

Megan McDonald also wrote a book about a hermit crab!

The Mermaid's Toenail

CHILLY

BRRR

FROSTY

0°C

BRISK

FREEZING

SO-SO

-10

10

-20

20

WARM

LOOK OUT!!!
IT'S GETTING
HOT IN HERE!

°F

FROSTY FREEZER
HARDWARE

MADE IN FROG NECK LAKE.VA

7 WH2O NEWS

PASSENGER'S SIDE

"3-D Me"

by Judy Moody

Most of the *NOT Bummer Summer* movie is live action, which means real kids and people act the parts. But there are a few places where you get to see what's inside my imagination! These scenes are done in 3-D animation by a company called Reel FX. They are super, way-cool famous for working on movies like *Bee Movie, Kung Fu Panda,* and *Open Season 2* and *3*!

And now they've turned me, Judy Moody, into a cartoon. They start out with a flat drawing of me from the Judy Moody books. Then they make a model of me on the computer. Next, they add movement, and before you know it, the cartoon me can walk across a tightrope! Magic! And guess what else? I *finally* have eyes, not just dots! I can blink! YAY!

Watch me go from this . . .

Fasten your seat belts! You won't believe *your* eyes when I go to Antarctica, cross the great Niagara Falls on a tightrope, or saw my best friend Rocky in half! Hardee-har-har! Even Mouse might have to close her eyes!

to THIS!

Judy "Scoops" Moody Talks to

JM: Ashley, you play the character of Jessica Finch in the movie version of my life. What do you and Jessica Finch have in common?

AB: *We both love pigs!*

JM: What's your favorite color?

AB: *Pink, of course! Same-same as Jessica Finch.*

JM: Are you an excellent speller like Jessica Finch?

AB: *I wish I could say yes, but not really. But I can spell HIPPOPONAMUS. (Look it up. See if I'm right.)*

JM: I know Jessica Finch would like to be in the Toad Pee Club. Are you in any clubs?

AB: *Yep! I'm in the Peegie Weegie Club. Anybody who can say Peegie Weegie can be in the club. (I would not want to be in the Gross Grub Club, even if you gave me a real-live potbelly pig.)*

JM: How old are you?

AB: *I just turned ten, so that puts me in the Double Digits Club, too. Ha!*

JM: Do you have any brothers or sisters?

AB: *Nope. I'm an only, and, yep, that's another club I'm in.*

JM: What do you like most about playing Jessica Finch?

AB: *The last character I played was a good girl. I like playing a character that does not have to be super-nice all the time.*

ASHLEY BOETTCHER (aka JESSICA FINCH)

JM: Do you have an idea for another Judy Moody movie?

AB: *You read my mind! In the next movie, Judy Moody and Jessica Finch should be zapped with a brain transplant. They just wake up one day, and—bam!—Jessica Finch's brain would be in Judy Moody's body and vice versa. It would be so funny and way confusing and mix everybody up.*

JM: Whoa!

Jessica's bike was decorated behind the scenes by Aimee O'Shea.

JESSICA FINCH'S MOVIE REVIEW

Judy Moody and the NOT Bummer Summer movie is a must-see, way-funny movie for kids and families. It is SO not just for girls. Boys are gonna love all the crazy action and comedy. Hardee-har-har! The roller coaster scene alone is worth the price of admission. I am N-O-T kidding. My favorite part is, of course, when I, Jessica Finch, get to ride the pink piggy bike and go faster than Humphrey, the Moody car. My UN-favorite part is that there are NO real-live PIGS in this movie, because I love-love-love pigs. (Even if there is a cat, a toad, an opossum, a macaw, four ponies, and an elephant.) Just wait for the sequel! And guess what—I am STILL not in the Toad Pee Club! No fair! Would someone PUH-LEASE talk to the writers? But don't be an aardwolf—go see this movie anyway! In a word, it's H-I-L-A-R-I-O-U-S! On a scale of 1 to 5, I give this movie **5 oinks!!**

"THERE ARE NO SMALL PARTS, ONLY SMALL ACTORS"

by Jessica Finch

I'm on screen for all of like three seconds. Doesn't seem like much, right? But think about it: if I hadn't been riding by on my bike at just the right moment, Judy and her aunt would never have been able to swipe it and use it to catch up with the ice-cream truck. If they hadn't been able to catch up to the ice-cream truck, the movie's key mysteries would never be solved! See what I mean? The point is, every single person is crucial to the success of the movie. Without me, the entire movie would have wobbled and fallen apart.

AND THE WINNER OF THE GIRAFFE AWARD IS . . .

Sarah Siegel-Magness! She is the Queen of Green. Sarah made the set of *Judy Moody and the NOT Bummer Summer* an earth-friendly one. Everyone even got their own reusable water bottle. How green was the Judy Moody set? I, Judy Moody, Garbologist, was on the case. Here's my way-official report. Check out all the stuff that got recycled in just *one* week on set! Not one single piece of garbage was sent to a landfill. Now that's *uber*-rare! No lie.

How much was recycled in one week?

- Bottles and cans: 72 pounds
- Cardboard: 231 pounds
- Paper: 61 pounds
- Compost (like ooey-gooey banana peels): 2180 pounds
- Metal: 64 pounds
- Green waste: 74 pounds

HELP HEAL THE WORLD!

The Environmental Media Association (EMA) has made it their mission to get folks in the entertainment industry to work in a more earth-friendly way. How? By giving out awards to the greenest of the green: actors, directors, studios, production companies, you name it.

Winners are announced at a special banquet every year. Doesn't that make you feel green with envy? At the awards banquet, organic food and drinks are served on chinaware (not paper or plastic!), reusable cloth banners and signs are used, and all paper materials are printed using soy-based ink on 100-percent recycled chlorine-free paper. And, of course, as much as possible is recycled.

"Never doubt that a small group of concerned people can change the world."

—**Margaret Mead**

Judy Moody Saves the World! *inspired Sarah Siegel-Magness to go green for the filming of* Judy Moody and the NOT Bummer Summer!

AN ALBUM

Hunter; Werewolf:
Cameron Boyce

WH2O Newscaster:
Jenn Korbee

Scream Monster ticket taker:
Pedro Shanahan

Maddy:
Ashley Jackson

Rocky's mom:
Jenica Bergere

Derrick, the surf instructor:
Frank Caronna

Movie ticket seller:
Norwood Cheek

Screaming woman
(AND executive producer!):
Bobbi Sue Luther

Rod Serling–type narrator:
James McManus

Zombie tourist:
Brian Palermo

Ivy, the movie ticket taker:
Megan Franich

Ringmaster:
Richard Riehle

John Schultz (center) confers with Richard Gibbs, composer (left), and Hal Olofsson (right), first assistant director.

Smile, Mrs. Frankenstein!

Stunt coordinator Joel Kramer with a couple of soggy actors

Jordana and Garrett show off their summer T-shirts.

Richard Haynes and Megan McDonald consult with Steve Gehrke, script supervisor.

Zombies like going to the movies, too.

Members of the Flip Club:
Taylar, Garrett, Cameron,
Preston, and Ashley

Animal handler
Shawn Webber
coaches Tux. Or
is that Tails?

John Schultz and Jody
Miller get in nice and
close for the scream!

Garrett Ryan with
Bobbi Sue Luther,
executive producer

★ ★ 133 ★ ★

John, is that you?

Kristoffer Winters and Janet Varney (aka Dad and Mom) ham it up.

Jordana and production assistant John Pace IV eye the surf.

Producer Sarah Siegel-Magness tries on Jody Miller's rig for size.

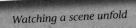

Watching a scene unfold

Eeeew! Is that ABC gum?

Parris gets Opalized!

Megan, Garrett, and Preston chat between takes.

"It's a wrap!"

ANSWER KEY

ANSWERS FROM PAGE 26

1. Mom

2. Dad

3. Dad

4. Mom

5. Mom

6. Mom

7. Dad

8. Dad

ANSWERS FROM PAGE 87

For each A answer, score 3
For each B answer, score 2
For each C answer, score 1

Add them all up. If you score 15–21, you are NOT a Fun Sponge. Five thrill points to you!

If you score 10–14, you are heading in the right direction but can sometimes be a Fun Rag or Fun Sponge.
Two thrill points for trying.

If you score less than 10, sorry, you are a Fun Mop! Subtract 3 thrill points!

(Don't forget to add your final total to your thrill points chart.)

SELECTED SOURCES

Stink's Film-O-Pedia
(pages 62–67)

http://www.filmsite.org/filmterms.html
http://www.imdb.com/glossary/

In a Same-Same Mood
(pages 76–77)

http://standincentral.com/2010/04/
28/interview-with-sarah-brynne/

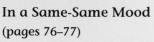

No Animals Were Harmed in the Making of this Film.
(pages 104–107)

http://www.americanhumane.org/
protecting-animals/programs/
no-animals-were-harmed/legacy-
of-protection.html

http://www.slate.com/id/2117565/

So You Want to Catch Bigfoot?
(pages 110–111)

Excerpt from *So You Want to Catch Bigfoot?* by Morgan Jackson with Jamie Michalak, illustrated by Mark Fearing (Candlewick Press, 2011).

"3-D Me" by Judy Moody
(pages 122–123)

http://www.radiumreelfx.com/entertainment

ACKNOWLEDGMENTS

The author and editor are grateful to the many people who so generously and patiently shared their time, energy, resources, and knowledge so that Judy Moody fans could take an amazing journey behind the scenes of *Judy Moody and the NOT Bummer Summer.* A very special thank-you to Sarah Siegel-Magness for saying "Yes" and and for saying "Welcome." Double high fives to the *uber*-awesome Bobbi Sue Luther, Richard Haynes, and Suzanne Tenner, who all went WAY above and beyond. Mega-thanks to Cynthia Charette, Don Diers, Mary Jane Fort, Tom Cahill, and Ben White for sharing their expertise and their enthusiasm.

It took an entire team of people to work on this and all of the Judy Moody movie tie-in books at Candlewick Press, but a special shout-out to Kristen Nobles, Lisa Rudden, and Liz Zembruski, as well as to Sally Bratcher, Maggie Deslaurier, Angela Dombroski, Martha Dwyer, Kate Fletcher, Gregg Hammerquist, Becky Hemperly, Kim Lanza, Karen Lotz, Hannah Mahoney, Mary McCagg, Heather McGee, Joan Powers, Peter H. Reynolds, Julianna Rose, Rachel Smith, Ann Stott, and Katie Warren.

Photo and Illustration Credits

All the photographs in this book were taken by Suzanne Tenner, set photographer, with the following exceptions:

Pages 10–13: professional head shots (center column of images) provided by Smokewood Entertainment

Pages 14, 112, 129, 137, and 142–143: book covers courtesy of Candlewick Press

Page 24: photo of Megan McDonald, Jordana Beatty, and Peter H. Reynolds courtesy of Smokewood Entertainment, taken by Nick Snyder

Pages 34–37: storyboards courtesy of Smokewood Entertainment, drawn by James Doh and Rod Douglas

Page 40: map of Frog Neck Lake courtesy of Smokewood Entertainment, designed by Lauren Day

Pages 41–43: house and creek location shots courtesy of Smokewood Entertainment, taken by Valerie Green and Kristi Frankenheimer

Pages 45, 48, 108, 118–121: logos, storefront designs, bumper stickers, and vehicle detail courtesy of Smokewood Entertainment

Page 48: painting of Larkspur Pier courtesy of Smokewood Entertainment, created by Cynthia Charette

Pages 80–81: Amy Namey's Video Diary images courtesy of Smokewood Entertainment, created by Lauren Day

Pages 123 and 137: animation cel courtesy of Smokewood Entertainment, created by Reel FX

Judy Moody and the NOT Bummer Summer

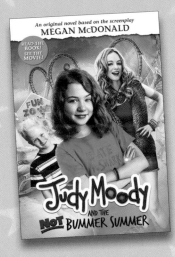

Roar! Just when it looks like Judy Moody's summer is going to be BOR-ing—eureka!— she comes up with the most thrill-a-delic plan ever. Get ready for a race involving tightropes, roller coasters, and zombies! Add in a hunt for Judy's teacher, an *uber*-adventurous aunt, a midnight stakeout, a runaway ice-cream truck, and a dash of Bigfoot, and what have you got? The Judy Moodiest summer ever!

By Megan McDonald, based on the screenplay by Kathy Waugh and Megan McDonald.
Features full-color stills from the movie

So You Want to Catch Bigfoot?

Stink is on high alert when several sightings of Bigfoot have been made in the neighborhood. To assist him in his search for the elusive creature, Aunt Opal gives Stink a copy of *So You Want to Catch Bigfoot?*

Now Judy Moody and Bigfoot fans alike can own a facsimile of this valuable field guide, containing everything you need to know about the furry fugitive, including tips on trapping and releasing your specimen.

by Morgan Jackson PhD with Jamie Michalak, illustrated in black and white by Mark Fearing

Need more Moody?

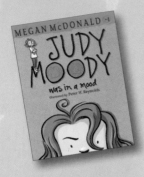

Celebrating 10 mega-

Try These!

Moody years. No lie!

★ ★ ★ Your Thrill Points! ★ ★ ★

Page #	Challenge	Possible Points	Your Points
25	Tongue Twister 1	3	
25	Tongue Twister 2	6	
26	Moody Squared	8	
27	Do Not Disturb	10	
33	John Schultz Movies	6	
40	Frog Neck Lake	2	
59	Bad Hair Day 1	3	
59	Bad Hair Day 2	5	
71	Summer Jobs 1	5	
71	Summer Jobs 2	10	
74	Backyard Circus	20	
80	Finding Borneo	2	
85	Roller Coaster 1	2	
85	Roller Coaster 2	5	
87	Fun Sponge	5	
97	Curl Shapes	61	
108	Bumper Stickers	2	
113	Read about Bigfoot	5	
116	Bigfoot Stakeout	20	
		180	

Total Possible Points

Your Big
Fat Total

THE MUSICIAN'S GUIDE TO THE

INTERNET

SECOND EDITION

BY

TODD SOUVIGNIER
& GARY HUSTWIT

©2002 Hal Leonard Corporation.

First Edition by Gary Hustwit
Second Edition by Todd Souvignier

Every effort has been made to provide correct information, however the publisher does not guarantee the accuracy of any material and does not assume responsibility for information included in or omitted from this publication. Inclusion in this publication does not constitute an endorsement or recommendation from the publisher, except where noted.

Digital photographs used in this publication have been downloaded from publicly accessible archives and are used in this publication for news reportage purposes only to demonstrate the variety of graphics available on the Internet. The source of each photograph is identified.

Gary thanks: Erica Schlaug, Salon.com, Denise Hustwit, William Hustwit, Brad Smith, Rob Levine, Apple Computer, and all the people who contributed information to this book.

Todd thanks: Steve Oppenheimer at Electronic Musician magazine, Dan Brown from Apple Computer, Brad Smith and Ben Schafer at HLC, Richard Lee, Brit Peddie, Thomas Dimuzio, Marco Gavini, Valentin Kantchev, Kalin Toshev, Gary Hustwit and Anne Souvignier.

Library of Congress Cataloging-in-Publication data has been applied for.

ISBN 0-634-01012-3

Published by Hal Leonard Corporation
7777 West Bluemound Road
P.O. Box 13819
Milwaukee, WI 53213, USA

Trade Book Division Editorial offices:
151 West 46th Street, 8th Floor
New York, NY 10036

Printed in the United States of America

10 9 8 7 6 5 4 3 2 1

Contents

Introduction   7

1. The Basics   9

2. Equipment Requirements   12

3. Getting Online   14

4. E-mail   16

5. Newsgroups and Mailing Lists   18

6. The World Wide Web   20

7. Chat, IRC and Instant Messaging   22

8. Preparing Music for the Web   24

9. MP3 and Compressed Audio   27

10. Hanging Your First Web Page   32

11. Creating Your Own Web Site   35

12. Internet Radio and Streaming Audio   43

13. File Sharing   49

14. Selling Music Online   57

15. Building Web Traffic   64

16. Conclusion   72

Appendix: Glossary   73

        Index   82

Introduction

Yes, the Internet is taking over the planet. Yes, it has changed the way we communicate. Yes, everyone's using it. And yes, you can use the Internet, if you're not already, to promote your music, make valuable contacts and further your musical career!

This book explains what the Internet is and how musicians can take advantage of it. We'll explain the linked networks of thousands of computers worldwide that make up the Internet, and the World Wide Web, the most popular area of the Internet.

Having an "official" artist Web site is a sign of credibility and proof that you are able to market and promote your music. By the time you finish this book you'll be able to create your own Web site! This page belongs to the band M.I.R.V. - http://www.mirv.com

The Web is used by individuals and institutions to publish content electronically. The Web is used by businesses to advertise every imaginable product and service. It's used by artists to create interactive, multimedia entertainment and education.

This book also explains some of the technospeak that you'll run into when you're online, and basically gives a crash course in Internet 101. We'll be touching on a lot of fairly complex subjects, some of which could (and do) have entire books written about them. This is *not* the definitive tech manual to the Internet. This book *is* designed to be a quick guide to getting online, and getting your music out there.

Music on the Net

Record labels, bands, music organizations, musical equipment manufacturers, promoters and music magazines are just some of the people and companies that use the Web to reach a global audience, 24 hours a day. That is

A Web site is your "space" on the Internet. A site is made up of "pages" of information. The first page people see when they visit your site is known as your "home page."

probably the biggest single advantage of the Internet: the ability to potentially reach millions of people, worldwide, easily and without having to shell out a huge amount of money. If you create your own World Wide Web "site," you can use it to play your music for people, promote upcoming events, or even sell your latest CD. You can distribute your music electronically to millions of potential listeners. If you don't already have a Web site for your band or business, starting one is easier and more affordable than you think.

There are tens of thousands of music-related Web sites and discussion groups on the Internet, and new ones are being added every day! We're going to focus on showing you how to establish a presence on the Internet, and how to make use of some of the key parts for musicians.

You do need to have some computer skills to use this book and get online. But even if you're a computer novice, you'll find that with a little bit of effort, navigating and using the Internet isn't hard. This isn't the *Computer Programmer's Guide to the Internet*, it's the **Musician's** *Guide to the Internet*. You're a musician (at least we hope you are), and you'd probably like to concentrate on your music and not on computer programming. For that reason we'll try to be as direct and clear as possible in this book. We'll skip the arcane technical data in favor of the easiest-way-to-do-it approach. Where possible we'll emphasize solutions that are either cheap or free.

Oh yeah, you'll also need a computer. See the Equipment Requirements in Chapter 2 for a rundown of what hardware you'll need to surf the Net.

Just like musical styles, the Internet is changing quickly, but the fundamentals remain the same. Getting a basic understanding of a few core things like FTP will only take a little while, and will open up all kinds of possibilities for you. Just like learning some new chords.

We've tried to make this book both current and timeless but things do change all the time. If you discover a Web site address in this book that no longer works, just slap the name of the company or product into any Search Engine and you'll surely pick up the trail.

When the first edition of this book was published (waaay back in 1997), putting music on the web was still a novelty. Now the large media companies are involved, as are millions of musicians and music fans worldwide.

There is a digital music revolution going on — you might have seen the headlines — we want to invite you to join in.

1.The Basics

What is the Internet?

The Internet ("Net" for short) is a huge network of thousands of computers worldwide that are hooked together via phone lines and other types of fancier connections. These computers are located at universities, government agencies, businesses and maybe even your next-door neighbor's house. They are all linked together, and each has been given a distinct address. You can think of the Internet as the hardware, the computers themselves and the phone lines. E-mail and the World Wide Web are just information that travels over this hardware, from your computer to others linked to the Net, and vice versa. This is a very simplified explanation, but you get the point.

E-mail

The number of e-mail messages sent each year far surpasses the number of standard letters sent via mail worldwide. We're talking billions per year. E-mail is easy, quick, and far-reaching. E-mail gives you the capability of sending messages to hundreds or thousands of people with just the click of a button, practically for free.

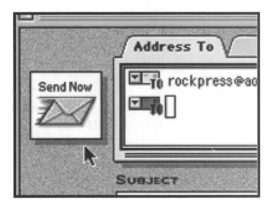

Just type your message and click send. That simplicity has made e-mail wildly popular.

Look at the math: If you're in a band, you know what a hassle it is to make 500 fliers (and pay for them), stick them in 500 envelopes, address them to 500 people on your mailing list and buy 500 stamps to send them out. That mailing will cost you $200 and a lot of time. If you had used an e-mail mailing list, you could have composed a message hyping your band's upcoming show, even pasted your poster art into the message, and clicked SEND. Your fans would get your message almost instantly, and they could even respond right back to you to ask how much the cover charge is. And that $200 you spent on the conventional mailing (snail mail) could've paid for an entire year's worth of dial-up Internet access.

Sure, snail mail still makes a more personal impression. Okay, so your fans don't get to hold that beautiful flier in their hands, or stick it on their refrigerator unless they print it out. Sometimes there is no substitute for paper-based correspondence. But for quick, cheap, global communication, there is no arguing that e-mail is the best way to go. See Chapters 4 and 15 for more information about e-mail plus strategies for using it effectively.

The World Wide Web

HTML: Hypertext Markup Language. This is the programming language used to make Web pages. Relax, it's easy to learn.

What people refer to as "the Web" is information stored on different computers on the Internet. These computers are called "servers" or "host computers" and they're set up so you can access them from your computer. The information they contain is formatted in a language called **HTML**. A World Wide Web browser program, like Netscape Navigator or Microsoft Internet Explorer, can read the HTML language and display the information on your computer. This information can be pictures, text, video clips, sound files, etc.

Web information is organized into "pages" — different sections that you can explore. Most Web pages have "links," which are areas you can click on that will guide you to another part of that Web site, or to any other Web site. A link could send your Web browser to an entirely different computer, in another part of the world, that is likewise linked to the Internet.

Web browsers give you graphical access to HTML data.

These links are why it's called "the Web" — because everything is inter-connected. You could be looking at the Web site of an independent record label in New York, and click on a link to one of their bands' Web sites in London. That band's site may have links to several other bands' sites, so you can check those out as well. Or maybe there's a link to a music magazine's site. And the magazine's site is linked to a tour site. And so on, and so on.

There is an incredible amount of free information and entertainment out there, and it's just a matter of exploring it. You can hang your own Web page, with information about you, your band or your music. Absolutely no programming is necessary; if you can click with a mouse you're practically already there. With a little elbow grease you can set up your own Web site, then you'll be linked into the intertwining circus called the Web.

Usenet Newsgroups and Mailing Lists

Usenet is a network of bulletin board services and computers that share discussion groups on thousands of different topics. The topics are broken down into "newsgroups," which are areas where users can add their opinions by adding (called "posting") articles to the newsgroup. These aren't articles in the traditional newspaper sense, they are comments and questions posted by the general public, not reporters. Newsgroups are not live discussions or chat areas. Using a program called a newsreader, you read articles that have been posted earlier, then post your response or comments.

There are newsgroups on everything from the care and breeding of chinchillas (alt.chinchilla) to even more esoteric subjects: techno-shamanism anyone? (alt.techno.shamanism) There are also hundreds of different music-related newsgroups, ranging from fans of specific artists (alt.music.abba) to music genres (alt.music.african).

Mailing Lists are sort of like newsgroups, but the discussion comes to you. Instead of posting articles to a newsgroup, the postings are sent to everyone who subscribes to the mailing list, and they in turn can add their comments by e-mailing their response to everyone else on the list. Like newsgroups, these mailing lists cover thousands of different topics, and people all over the world participate in them.

See Chapter 5 for more about how to participate in Usenet newsgroups and mailing lists.

FTP

FTP stands for *File Transfer Protocol*. It's a method of downloading files from other computers on the Net. Transferring files from one machine to the other is basically all the Internet consisted of until the emergence of the World Wide Web. There are FTP sites where you can download applications, text documents and other information you may be looking for. When you set up your own Web site you'll use FTP to place your music and Web pages on a Web server.

Most Web browser programs include basic FTP capabilities, so you could use a browser like Netscape Navigator or Microsoft Internet Explorer to download from FTP sites if you need to. To do any real work you'll need a program called an "FTP client," which makes it easy to download or upload files. Examples of FTP clients include Fetch on the Macintosh and FTP Voyager for Windows.

FTP Voyager is an example of an FTP client program.

Internet Terms

Okay, so there's a ton of jargon associated with the Internet. Yes, it's scary, so we'll devote a few pages to some of the basic slang and technospeak. Have a look at the Glossary, located at the back of this book. It is a sampling of terminology that you'll run into as you're learning about the Internet and the World Wide Web.

2.Equipment Requirements

Computers

If you don't already have a computer, you'll need a Macintosh or Windows PC with at least 64 megabytes of RAM and a hard drive (the bigger the better). Sixty-four megs of RAM is the bare minimum these days; RAM has come way down in price and if you can afford more, get it. Usually any PC that can run Windows 95 or later, or any Mac running at least MacOS 7.5, will be able to launch a browser and get connected to the Net.

Modems

Your modem is your vehicle for online transportation. Modem speed is measured in BPS, or bits per second. Almost any new computer you buy these days comes bundled with a 56,000 bps modem, and will work for standard e-mail, newsgroups and Web browsing.

56,000 bps (also written as **56 kbps** or simply **56k**) is the *minimum* acceptable modem speed. There are a lot of old 14,400 and 28,800 bps (14.4 and 28.8 kbps) modems floating around, but don't bother with them, they're too slow for Web browsing.

Conventional modems connect to the Internet using a standard telephone line; this is referred to as a "dial-up" connection.

Broadband

ISDN was the original broadband service, it offered speeds up to 128,000 bps. Unfortunately ISDN was pretty expensive and not widely deployed. It kind of got eclipsed by DSL and Cable modem.

Cable modem is offered by cable TV companies. They'll give you a special modem that hooks up to a coaxial cable. Cable modems typically download at speeds ranging from 400,000 bps (400kbps) to 1.5Mbps (1,500,000 bps) with uploading speeds between 100 and 200kbps. Cable modem systems are laid out in such a way that the users must share upload and download bandwidth with their neighbors, a key distinguishing point between it and DSL. Sharing bandwidth isn't a big deal until lots of your neighbors get Cable modem, then things start to really slow down.

DSL, short for Digital Subscriber Line, is offered by a number of firms including major phone companies. The most common type of DSL takes advantage of unused wires found in most phone systems.

Garden variety DSL is simple enough for most people to install unaided; you're provided with a DSL modem and some filters that are snapped onto the household phone jacks. Plug the phones back in, hook up the modem to the computer and away you go.

DSL speeds vary, 128kbps upstream and 512kbps to 1.5Mbps (1,500,000 bps) downstream are typical. DSL can go much faster; download speeds of up to 6,100,000 bps (6.1Mbps) are possible but may cost more and you have to be close to their central office. Although DSL utilizes phone wiring it doesn't tie up your phone line like a dial-up modem.

"Fixed wireless" and satellite DSL services are also available; both use a microwave dish pointed at a distant receiver. You'll need a clear line-of-sight to a local tower to qualify for fixed wireless; nearby trees and large buildings scuttle many attempted installations. Another issue with fixed wireless is that upload bandwidth is shared among the users of each receiver, kind of like cable.

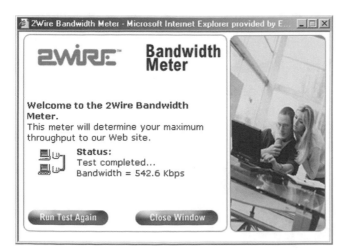

Check your broadband speed by using a modem test page. This one is at http://www.2wire.com

The Waiting

With a 56k modem, you'll be waiting up to a half hour for a typical three-minute MP3 file to download. If you've got the money, splurge on broadband. You'll be able to download an MP3 in two or three minutes.

Faster types of broadband such as T-1 and T-3 service are available but are found mostly in businesses due to their higher cost and complexity.

There is heavy competition for broadband customers in the densely populated regions of the U.S., which makes it easier to get a good deal. We were able to convince Cable modem and DSL providers to waive the set-up fees, and provide the modems and filters free of charge, just by asking.

13

3. Getting Online

Once you have your equipment squared away, it's time to get "wired." You have options when it comes to getting access to e-mail, newsgroups and the Internet. The main ones are Online Services (like America Online or the Microsoft Network) and what we'll call "straight" Internet access, through a local Internet Service Provider (ISP). They both have their strengths and weaknesses. Another option is to get access through a school, university, library or business if you can.

Online Services

Companies like America Online and the Microsoft Network have earned millions of subscribers by offering e-mail and access to the Web, plus their own, proprietary content. Everything from weather reports to major online magazines to forums and discussion groups on thousands of subjects are provided by these companies for their subscribers only. While the World Wide Web is free and open to everyone, **Online Services** are accessible only to the people that pay a monthly fee, usually around $20.

America Online's Web entrance. AOL's ease of use has made it the most popular Online Service.

Basically, these services have "packaged" the Internet experience, and try to make it easy for newcomers to get online. They offer dial-up service that will work with any 56k modem, plus an e-mail account, Web access, exclusive content and other stuff.

We like AOL's ease of use, Instant Messaging, Chat and loads of special interest channels. Their e-mail system is extremely simple to use; you'll literally be up and running in a few minutes. AOL has a large music section, with tons of music-related discussion groups and industry-sponsored areas. AOL also offers free Web pages to its members; you'll still need to set up your page, but they offer pointers there, too. If you're intimidated by this Internet stuff, AOL is probably the most-assisted way to test the waters. Internet training wheels, if you will.

If you aren't interested in their content, don't require all the help or just don't dig Microsoft and AOL, call an ISP.

"Straight" Internet Access

The Online Services hold your hand. Internet Service Providers (**ISP**s) just give you access; they mostly skip the special content and custom-branded services. You can find Internet Service Providers in your Yellow Pages or in a local computer magazine. These companies give you straight, unfiltered access to the Internet, for anywhere from $10 per month and up. ISPs are also in the hosting business, if you want to build your own Web site they can rent you space on their servers.

If you don't already have e-mail and browser software, the ISP will give it to you and the installations are pretty self-explanatory. The things to remember (and write down in a safe place) are:

- Your **User Name** and **Password**

- **PPP** server — the name of a computer that holds your incoming e-mail, typically something like mail.ispcompany.com

- **SMTP** server — the computer that takes your outgoing e-mail, usually a name like smtp.ispcompany.com

The ISP is also going to assign you an **IP address**. This is the unique Internet Protocol address for your computer. In most cases it's assigned "dynamically," meaning it's different every time you connect. A "static" IP address is one that stays fixed, commonly seen with Cable modems.

When selecting an ISP your choices boil down to dial-up (56k modem) and broadband (Cable modem or DSL.) Find the cheapest dial-up account and start *now* if that's all you can afford. If you can possibly spring for it, broadband's what you want. Broadband isn't available everywhere and your service choices may be limited by your locale.

The next few chapters will give you more information on how to get these applications to get access to the most popular and useful features of the Internet: using e-mail, mailing lists, newsgroups, the World Wide Web and file sharing. Once you have Internet access you're ready to proceed. Remember that the best source of information about getting online is other people who've done it. Don't be afraid to ask your friends, relatives or other musicians how they got set-up and how they're using the Net.

4.E-mail

Electronic mail is the easiest and most useful tool for musicians and music-related businesses. It also works great for staying in touch with far-away pals! Every day, millions of e-mail messages are criss-crossing the Internet.

The ISP or online service will give you basic e-mail software, or you can download any popular e-mail program from the Web.

If you're running Windows, it features a built-in e-mail program called Microsoft Outlook Express, and an upgrade pro version called simply Outlook. Netscape's Navigator browser has a built-in mail program and there are also many "stand alone" e-mail programs.

Most online services and ISPs let you choose your own e-mail address. It must be unique, just like your normal street address (or "snail mail" address), and consist of several parts, or domains. For example, Todd's address is **todds@neteze.com**. So each address consists of a user name (or screen name) and the @ "at" symbol, followed by the name of the host computer and then the dot-com, which is the "top level domain" designation for a commercial, for-profit company.

You'll see various e-mail addresses with different top-level domains that indicate what type of organization runs that host computer. **edu** stands for educational (computers at schools), **gov** is government, **net** is a network or information center, **org** is a non-profit organization and **mil** is the U.S. Military. Foreign countries also have a two-letter designation for their particular country, as in **se** for Sweden (e.g. fountain@algonet.se).

E-mail Strategies

The best features of e-mail programs are the **CC** (carbon copy) and **BCC** (blind carbon copy) functions. These allow you to send one message to several, or several hundred, people at once. The CC function allows the recipients to see who else got your message, but the BCC command hides the names of the recipients from each other. Careless (or malicious) people who are responding to your message can send their response to your entire mailing list if you only CC it. Always use BCC when doing mass mailings.

Obviously, the best use of these carbon copy functions is a mailing list of friends or fans. If you perform live, start asking people who come to your shows for their e-mail addresses. You'll soon amass a sizeable e-mailing list, which will make it easy (and cheap) to update everyone you know online about upcoming shows, record releases, news, or updates to your Web site. In addition to sending text messages, you can paste pictures into the e-mail message or send an entire Web page. Be cautious about sending large attached documents or files, people don't appreciate unexpected huge downloads.

Solicited vs. SPAM

Another rule in e-mail etiquette (or Netiquette) is that if you don't know someone, and they didn't specifically ask you to, don't include them in your e-mail list. Unsolicited e-mail is like junk mail (at least it doesn't destroy trees.) People's reactions to it can be just as negative. Junk e-mail, also called **Spam**, is generally viewed as an annoyance. Spamming also refers to posting sales-pitch-type messages on Usenet newsgroups or posting messages that have nothing to do with that newsgroup's topic.

If you decide to be a Spammer, brace yourself for some flames. Note that certain ISPs will kick persistant Spammers off their networks if people are complaining.

Smile When You Say That!
Some sample emoticons:

:-)	*smile*
;-)	*smile w/wink*
:-(	*frown*
B-)	*smile with glasses*
8-)	*wide-eyed smile*
:-D	*laughing*
:-o	*Mr. Bill*
:-P	*tongue sticking out*
:-J	*tongue in cheek*
:-$	*sick person*
@:-\	*Elvis*

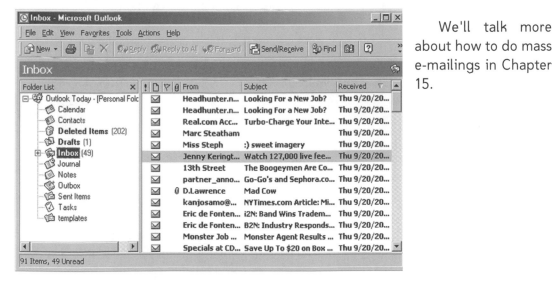

We'll talk more about how to do mass e-mailings in Chapter 15.

Microsoft Outlook is a well-known e-mail program. Outlook Express is the junior version.

5.Newsgroups and Mailing Lists

Usenet

Usenet is a worldwide distributed discussion system. It consists of a set of topics, called **newsgroups**, with names that are classified by subject. There are thousands of different newsgroups on almost every conceivable subject possible, with people engaging in online discussions about common interests. "Articles" or "messages" are "posted" to these newsgroups by people all over the world.

Some newsgroups are "moderated;" in these newsgroups, the articles are first sent to a moderator for approval before appearing in the newsgroup. Like the Internet, no person or group has authority over Usenet as a whole. You're on your own.

Your ISP or online service should carry all the newsgroups on Usenet. To read Usenet newsgroups, you can use either a stand-alone newsreader program, a Web browser that has newsreader capability (most do) or go through a commercial online service like AOL. You "subscribe" to a newsgroup by selecting it with your newsreader. The next time you check, your newsreader will show you all the new postings in that newsgroup since you last looked at it.

Newsgroups are organized into different subject categories called "hierarchies." These are at the beginning of each newsgroup's name; for example, **comp.fonts**. The **comp** stands for computer-related, and the **fonts** stands for digital typefaces (see sidebar for more hierarchies.) At first glance, you might not understand some of the articles in the newsgroups. Usenet veterans have their own jargon and abbreviations, and most postings are responses to previous postings that you may not have seen. This series of articles and replies to those articles is referred to as a thread. The best way to familiarize yourself with newsgroups is to "lurk" for a while, that is, read them but don't post any articles yourself. The vast majority of people on Usenet are lurkers rather than posters.

A few Usenet "hierarchies" or main categories:

comp	*Computers*
misc	*Miscellaneous*
news	*News and info about Usenet*
rec	*Recreational*
sci	*Science*
talk	*Discussion of issues*
alt	*Alternative*

As of this writing there are more than 600 different newsgroups under the alt.music category alone, with hundreds of thousands of articles.

Once you start reading newsgroups, you won't believe the amount of information and forums that are out there. Some of them are useful, and some are just plain wastes of cyberspace. Subscribe to a few that sound interesting, and go from there.

Google Groups

A great way to search Usenet newsgroups for names or topics is by going to **Google Groups** (http://groups.google.com). Having acquired the old DejaNews Usenet archive, Google lets you search virtually all of Usenet for any word or subject. This works well if you want to find out if anyone is talking (good or bad) about you or your band in any of the newsgroups.

The Google Groups Web site lets you quickly search through Usenet newsgroups.

Mailing Lists

Mailing Lists are a lot like newsgroups in the sense that they are open discussion groups on specific topics that you can participate in. But instead of posting to Usenet, the discussions are sent to you via e-mail. When you post an article to a mailing list, your message is going to everyone on the list, and vice versa. If you just got your e-mail account set up and you want to receive some mail, subscribe to a mailing list — you'll get plenty. Some mailing lists eventually become Usenet newsgroups.

There is just as diverse and numerous an array of topics for mailing lists as there is for newsgroups. For directories of mailing lists and information on how to subscribe to lists, check out http://paml.net or http://www.liszt.com.

Acronyms you may run across on Usenet:

FAQ	*Frequently-Asked Questions*
BTW	*By The Way*
FWIW	*For What It's Worth*
IMO	*In My Opinion*
LOL	*Laughing Out Loud*

6.The World Wide Web

The Web is the most exciting part of the Internet and its global impact is demonstrated by the millions of people who are staring at their computer screens as you read this, jumping from Web site to Web site, soaking up the online information like so many caffeine-driven sponges. The capacity for people to easily publish digital content on the Web has led to an explosion of instantly accessible information about any subject you're interested in.

Once you're able to access the Web, you'll be floored by the amount of amazing (sometimes ridiculous) information that's on it. It really is revolutionary when it comes to quickly researching almost anything. With search engines like Yahoo! we were able to find relatives that our immediate families never knew we had by searching for "Hustwit" and "Souvignier." If you're trying to locate a company but maybe only know the name of their product, or the type of product, you can quickly find the company, its address, phone number, directions to its headquarters and even its competitors. Those are only two quick examples. There is an endless amount of stuff on the Web and most users get addicted.

Internet Explorer is Microsoft's World Wide Web browser.

Web Browsers

The first step in getting on the Web is getting a **Web browser** program. Arguments over which Web browser is superior are best left to the computer industry magazines and the software companies that make the browsers. In the interests of speed and simplicity, we're going to recommend that you use either Microsoft **Internet Explorer** or Netscape's **Navigator** browser (also bundled as Netscape Communicator.) Both work well, are available free and are compatible with nearly every one of the millions of Web pages on the Internet. They're also very easy to use. Just type in the address (URL) of the Web site you want to check out, and in a few seconds you're there.

Netscape and Internet Explorer both have FTP and newsreader capabilities, Netscape also includes a built-in e-mail program. You can download

Web Surfing Tip:

Due to the increasing traffic and inherent inconsistency of the Internet, you'll sometimes get "server not responding" and "server does not have a DNS entry" errors when you're trying to access a site. Try again a few seconds later, and keep trying. Many times you'll get through on the third or fourth try.

the latest versions for Mac or PC at http://home.netscape.com or http://www.microsoft.com/downloads. This is sort of a chicken and egg situation, because if you don't already have a browser, you can't go to their Web site to download one! Fortunately most new computers have one or both browsers pre-installed and most ISPs distribute a browser on their setup discs.

There are books available about each browser that specifically explain the details of that browser and other Internet-related software. Shop around if you're looking for more in-depth information, but again, browsers are very easy to use and learn.

Search Engines

Once you get your Web browser up and running, where do you go? A great first site to check out is a search engine such as **Yahoo!** at http://www.yahoo.com. Search Engines are huge directories that list other Web sites, thousands of them, usually indexed into easy-to-use categories: entertainment, sports, politics, art, etc. There are dozens of search engines out there; we like Yahoo, **Google** (http://www.google.com) and **Dogpile** (http://www.dogpile.com).

Yahoo has a lot of well-organized music content.

There are a zillion Web pages on the Internet, but none so interesting as your own. We'll show you how to hang a simple Web page at any band site in Chapter 10, how to create your own personal Web site in Chapter 11 and how to get listed in Search Engines in Chapter 15. Don't worry, it's all really easy.

7. Chat, IRC and Instant Messaging

Chat

IRC, or **Internet Relay Chat**, is a network of servers on the Net that host "**chat**" areas. These are free-form, un-moderated, real-time discussions referred to as "channels." What you type on the screen in these "discussion rooms" is instantly visible to everyone else involved in the discussion, and vice-versa.

At any given moment there are thousands of online live chats underway, on thousands of different subjects or on no subject at all. Many of them are on IRC, but commercial online services have hundreds of "chat rooms" as well. The difference is that while IRC is open to everyone on the Net, chat areas on commercial services like America Online and the Microsoft Network are available only to their subscribers.

To access IRC, you'll need a client program. Two venerable shareware IRC programs are: **Ircle** for Macintosh (available at http://www.ircle.com) and **mIRC** for Windows (http://www.mirc.com.) Both programs give you easy access to most of the world's IRC action. You'll need to log-on to an IRC server; try to pick one close to your geographical area. Once you're logged-on, you can access all the channels on all the other servers as well. When you join a channel you'll be able to see who else is involved in the chat, and you can also invite other people online to a private conversation or send private messages to other chat participants.

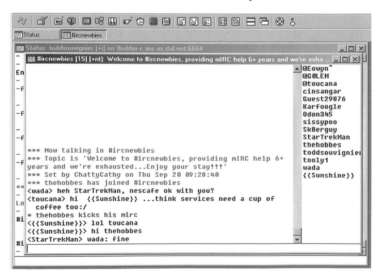

mIRC is a well-known and simple-to-use IRC client

Be forewarned that anything goes on IRC; the most popular channels are devoted to sex. There are lots of music-related discussions, however, and using IRC is a cheap and easy way to do "live" online chats by your band or artists on your label. Just announce the time and channel name of your live interview on your Web site a few weeks in advance. Obviously anyone who wants to participate in the chat will need to have IRC software as well, so put a link on your page to the Ircle and mIRC sites mentioned above.

Instant Messaging

Instant Messaging is a little like e-mail, a little like chat. Instant Messaging allows you to pass notes with your circle of friends in real-time. Discussions take place on a private channel. Over time you'll build up a Contact List or Address Book that contains the Instant Messaging addresses and identities of your friends.

AOL Instant Messenger is one of AOL's marquee features. Some users hang on to their AOL service just so they can stay in contact with their Buddy List. Naturally, Microsoft has its own **MSN Messenger Service** (http://messenger.msn.com).

ICQ ("I Seek You") is another popular Instant Messaging program, boasting more than 100 million users. It's owned by AOL and is still available free from http://web.icq.com.

Instant Messaging is a terrific thing for bands, small businesses, families and other special interest groups, especially when collaborating on projects. You can stay in constant, real-time communication or you can just leave notes when people are logged-out or away from the computer.

Microsoft's MSN Messenger Service makes it easy to add any Hotmail or MSN user to your contact list.

8.Preparing Music for the Web

There are several ways to expose your music to the Net masses. The easiest way is to digitize it and put it on your Web site as a downloadable audio file. Users can grab these sound files and play them on their computers but due to the large size such downloads may take a while. A slightly more complicated way is to offer streaming audio on your Web site. With streaming, Web surfers do not have to go through the time-consuming process of downloading the entire audio file before they can listen to it. They can listen to the music as it is being downloaded, without the wait. The sound files are transferred and played in a continuous "stream."

Sonic Foundry's Sound Forge is a robust, professional audio editor for Windows.

Most Internet audio is "compressed" to decrease the file size and make downloading or streaming easier. We'll cover compression schemes including MP3 in the next chapter. In this chapter we discuss how to get your music onto your computer and how to prepare it for compression and Internet distribution.

Uncompressed CD-quality audio (a WAV, AIFF or SD2 file) takes up about 10MB per stereo track minute. A three-minute song is around 30MB.

If you use a Windows PC, you'll be creating files in the **WAV** audio file format. Mac users work with either **AIFF** or Sound Designer II (**SD2**) file formats. These are all uncompressed, "raw" audio file formats, which allow you to do substantial editing and processing to the sound, unlike compressed formats such as MP3.

Digitizing Your Music

The sound quality of the finished audio file largely depends on the quality of the original recording and how it is input into the computer. If you have your music on a compact disc and your computer has a CD-ROM drive, you can import a song directly from your CD using sound-editing or player/encoder software. Importing from CD is the easiest and best-sounding method of getting your music onto your computer; you're simply copying the bits to your hard drive.

If your music is on a DAT, cassette or vinyl, you'll have to patch an output cord from your stereo into the "sound in" port on your sound card. All contemporary Macs and PCs have built-in 16-bit stereo sound cards, which ostensibly offer "CD-Quality" audio and can be used successfully for recording music onto your computer. Actual sound quality will vary; the sound cards built into most laptops are noticeably noisy, and you'll always suffer a quality loss whenever you record through any 1/8-inch stereo microphone jack.

For better recording quality consider an add-on sound card. Cards that will perform to professional standards start at around $200 and have higher quality RCA, balanced 1/4-inch or XLR inputs.

No matter how you acquire your audio, you're going to need ample hard drive space for the huge uncompressed sound files you'll be making.

You'll also need some type of sound editing software. There are excellent shareware programs like Felt Tip Software **Sound Studio** for Macintosh (http://www.felttip.com) or **Cool Edit 2000** "evaluation version" for Windows (http://www.syntrillium.com) For simple recording, the shareware programs can fill the bill and are an okay choice for a tight budget.

If you're doing lots of signal processing, as we'll discuss later in this chapter, you'll want a full-featured professional audio editor, like the upgrade version of Cool Edit, Sonic Foundry's **Sound Forge** for Windows (http://www.sonicfoundry.com) or Bias **Peak** for Mac (http://www.bias-inc.com.)

Digidesign offers a free version of their Pro Tools multi-track recording software for Mac and Windows. It allows you to do recording and signal processing as well as layering and mixing. Pro Tools is the digital recording system most commonly found in professional music and film sound studios, at least in the U.S., so it's a good one to know. If you can handle the complexity of this program (compared to editors like Peak or Sound Forge), **Pro Tools FREE** is certainly priced right (http://www.digidesign.com/ptfree).

Once you've imported or recorded your song and saved it to your hard drive as a WAV, AIFF or SD2 audio file, you can use your sound editing software to prepare it for Internet distribution.

CD-quality audio is 16-bit stereo, sampled at 44.1kHz. For best quality and ease of use always record at 16-bit, 44.1k.

Digidesign Pro Tools FREE is an eight-track version of their industry-standard multi-track audio editing and sequencing program.

File Preparation

Crop: Select and delete any extraneous noises like needle drops, count-ins or the tail end of the preceding song.

Insert Silence: Insert one or two seconds of silence at the very beginning of the song. This reduces the chance of stuttering when the player is launching and buffering.

EQ: Use an Equalizer to reduce or eliminate the highest and lowest frequencies in your song. "Rolling-off" the bass below 50Hz and the high end above 15kKz should have little noticeable impact on your sound, and will greatly reduce "aliasing" or distortion when you compress the audio. We're often more aggressive with the EQ — eliminating everything below 100Hz and above 12kHz in some cases — let your ears be your guide.

Remove DC Offset: Many recordings from turntable or cassette suffer from "DC Offset," a noticeable displacement of the audio into the positive or negative range, resulting from mismatched voltages. If your waveform looks like it's mostly in the top or bottom half of the display, use the "Remove DC Offset" function found in most audio editors.

Stereo To Mono: Converting Stereo to Mono reduces the file size by one-half. Of course, you lose any stereo image, but most listeners won't notice.

Limit: If your song has been professionally mastered, you probably don't need any limiting. However, if your music has not yet been mastered, or if it contains noticeable variations between loud and soft passages, you may want to apply some gentle limiting to smooth out the volume levels.

Normalize: Normalize is a simple way of making the entire file louder. Don't normalize to 100% if you're planning on compressing your audio — use a lower setting, from 95% to 99%.

One of the secret weapons of Internet Audio is a piece of software called **L1**, made by Waves (http://www.waves.com.) The L1 "UltraMaximizer" basically makes everything as loud as possible. L1 plugs-in to any professional sound editing or multi-track recording software. It's not cheap, but it really works and the results can be profound.

Now that you have a clean, digital copy of your song that has been edited and prepared, you're ready to encode it into a compressed format for Internet distribution. Read on to Chapter 9 to learn how!

9. MP3 and Compressed Audio

File **Compression**, the topic of this chapter, is not to be confused with audio signal compression, as one would do with a compressor-limiter. File Compression is about packing a large file down into a smaller size. It's a big deal because it makes it possible to distribute music over the Net without really long downloads.

Archive Utilities such as Stuffit or Winzip represent a type of file compression frequently encountered on the Internet for purposes other than music. Such programs are widely used when transmitting large documents or graphics. They make a compressed copy of any file — an Archive — and they also de-compress Archives so the contents can be used.

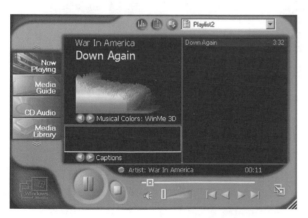

Microsoft's Windows Media Player is a free MP3 and WMA player for Windows and Mac.

Audio File Compression works in a comparable way. Programs called **Encoders** are used to compress the music. Listeners need to have a **Player**, a program that can unpack the compressed file and play the music. Compression/decompression schemes are called **codecs** for short.

MP3, WMA and other audio codecs take advantage of one of those quirks of human hearing, a phenomenon called "masking." Masking happens when loud sounds overshadow or drown out weaker sounds. Assuming listeners aren't going to notice or miss the masked sounds, the system uses more bits to represent prominent parts of the signal, and fewer bits to represent masked portions. Most of the music compression schemes in use today are variations on this technique, which is known as "Perceptual coding."

We're talking about throwing away data in such a way that you still have a reasonable representation of the original sound, but a much smaller file.

"Rip" (as in rip-off) means making a compressed file from a CD track. It's another word for Encoding.

Perceptual coding works pretty well but still causes a real reduction in the sound quality at moderate compression levels and can easily introduce distortion ("aliasing") at extreme settings.

Before you compress your own music you should understand some of the main characteristics that all compressed audio files share:

File Size

A compressed audio file is much smaller than the uncompressed original audio. As we mentioned in the previous chapter, CD-quality WAV, AIFF or SD2 files take up approximately 10MB of disk space per minute. A compressed file may be one-tenth that size, around 1MB per minute, or even smaller.

Bit Rate

Sound Quality = **Bit Rate**. The bigger the number, the higher the quality. Bit rate is a throughput measurement; it's the number of bits that must go through your player each second for the audio to be heard. Bit rate is measured in kilobits (thousands of bits) per second, or kbps for short. That's also how modem speed is measured (see Chapter 2).

128kbps is a typical bit rate for downloadable MP3 files. For low-fidelity streams, 24kbps is a rule-of-thumb bit rate.

Files with higher bit rates take more disk space; one minute of 64kbps music is half the size of a minute of 128kbps audio.

Bit rate is especially important with streaming audio. 56k modems rarely establish connections faster than 33kbps. Streams with bit rates higher than 32kbps will constantly exhibit varying degrees of delay or interruption during playback with dialup modems.

Tags

Also known as Metadata, **Tags** are descriptive text notes that are part of a compressed file. Tags hold information like Song Title, Artist Name, Album Title and Genre; in some cases they can contain detailed descriptions or even graphics. Tags are saved in the "header" of a compressed file, and take up very little space compared to the audio. Most players and some File Sharing programs recognize Tags.

Mono/Stereo

Mono means one-channel; the same audio is played in the left and right speakers. **Stereo** is two-channel, with separate signals for L and R. A 128kbps stereo file uses 64kbps to represent each channel. Therefore a 64kbps mono file has the same general audio fidelity as a 128kbps stereo file (albeit with no stereo image) and is only half the size. If you don't mind losing your stereo spread, consider encoding in mono.

Now that you have a handle on compression fundamentals, let's move on to examining some of the most popular codecs.

MP3

MP3 is an abbreviation for MPEG-1 Audio Layer 3. The Moving Picture Experts Group was a bunch of smart people, charged with the task of making audio/video content smaller. The audio portion of their specification has several "layers," each an encoding scheme of increasing fidelity and complexity. Audio Layer 3, or MP3, offers better quality than MP1 and MP2.

Of course the Moving Picture Experts didn't cook this up entirely out of the goodness of their hearts, they worked for companies that stood to benefit from the innovation. MP3 technology is licensed to other manufacturers by

MusicMatch Jukebox was one of the first MP3 player/encoders and is still a contender.

the Fraunhofer Institute in Germany. Their deal is that the players (decoding) can be freely distributed. But manufacturers have to pay if they want MP3 encoding in their products. Some software developers have paid Fraunhofer a sizeable flat licensing fee and can give away their encoders for free if they want (Apple iTunes, for example). Other developers pay an incremental fee for each encoder sold.

MP3 has been around for many years and is not the best-sounding or most versatile format available. Nevertheless, it became a very popular format and helped get the digital music revolution kick-started.

MP3 encoders have a couple advanced settings that bear mentioning:

CBR/VBR - CBR stands for Constant Bit Rate, indicating that the bit rate (kbps) will remain constant or steady throughout the file. Most MP3s encountered in the wild are encoded CBR. VBR means Variable Bit Rate, which uses fewer bits during simple or quiet passages. As a sound quality/file size improver, VBR is fairly ineffective. Moreover, some player/encoders and online music portals can't handle VBR files, so CBR is the safe choice.

Joint Stereo - An alternate stereo scheme that only gives improvements at low bit rates. Leave it on regular stereo.

Most band sites, including MP3.com, only accept Stereo files. However, if you're distributing music through a file sharing service or from your own Web site, anything goes. Since they can be half the size of Stereo, using Mono files will speed everything along.

There are two flavors of Tags for MP3 files, called **ID3v1** and **ID3v2**, version 2 allowing considerably more track information. Better encoders support both types.

One of the big things missing from MP3 is copy protection. There is no convenient way to control the use or distribution of an MP3 file, because there are no provisions for Digital Rights Management (**DRM**) in the MPEG-1 specification. This is one of the reasons MP3s are so popular with consumers.

You can create a streaming MP3 file, called a **M3U** — we'll explain how to do that in Chapter 12.

WMA

Short for Windows Media Audio, **WMA** is Microsoft's response to MP3. WMA files have better sound than MP3s at the same bit rates. Microsoft gives away the Windows Media Player and Windows Media Encoder, and licenses them to other developers free of charge.

WMA is attractive to record labels because it includes support for Digital Rights Management, allowing copyright owners to place restrictions on usage and distribution. WMA also offers the ability to insert URL scripts into a file, so that playing a song will cause Web pages to appear. We'll talk more about DRM in Chapter 14, and URL scripts in Chapter 15.

To stream a WMA you make a file called an **ASX**; see Chapter 12 for details.

Liquid Audio

Liquid Audio was the first compressed audio format to have a built-in security layer. Liquid was also early with adding album art, lyrics and liner notes to the audio file, so listeners could have a more complete experience. Liquid Audio has not become a dominant format with either consumers or copyright owners thus far; in fact, the Liquid Player now supports the competing MP3 and WMA formats.

A few years back Liquid took a whirl at offering encoding and hosting services to independent musicians but that initiative was short-lived; at present Liquid's business is oriented toward record labels and retailers.

Other Compressed Formats

There are lots of other compression schemes, including Dolby **AC3**, Sony **ATRAC3** and many others. Some like AT&T's **A2B** Music and Lucent's **ePAC** are already consigned to the dustbin of history. As we go to press, newcomers include the open-source **Ogg Vorbis** format (looks promising at this point) and Fraunhofer's own **mp3PRO**, which is not so hot in our opinion. Other formats will come along in the future. Owing to their pervasiveness, MP3 and WMA will probably be around for awhile.

Selecting A Format

Ease of distribution is the main consideration. Listeners must have player software installed on their computer that supports the format your music is in. MP3 players are prevalent among both Mac and Windows users, and most people who listen to Internet music have one. Macintosh users are generally less likely to have Windows Media Player installed, although it does run on Mac and is distributed free of charge.

WMA has better marketing-related features. Unfortunately, it's presently beyond the means of the average musician to make use of the DRM capabilities (Windows Media Rights Manager) to protect and control one's own songs. There's just no cheap and easy way to create your own "pay for download" or subscription setup, and no one at present is offering an inexpensive turnkey service that independent musicians could simply plug into. If giving away your music is a problem for you or your band, turn to Chapter 12 to learn about secure streaming audio.

Choosing An Encoder

As mentioned before, Apple iTunes is available free to Mac users, and runs on a G3 or faster. MusicMatch Jukebox and RealJukebox are also popular MP3 encoders, and both require payment after a certain point. Windows Media Encoder is free for Windows users. MP3.com has an extensive software section with reviews and trial versions of all the latest Encoders and Players and there's a ton of them — so check it out!

10. Hanging Your First Web Page

Once your music is in an Internet-ready format (such as MP3), you can start putting it on the Internet.

The easiest way to begin building your Web presence is to create pages at a **band site**. These sites, such as MP3.com, IUMA and many others, feature music and information from thousands of different independent bands and musicians, typically arranged by genre. They offer artists simple, automatic ways of building pages that can feature music, pictures, lyrics and lots of other information. In less than an hour you can create a Web page for your music, then invite others to view and listen.

A band page at IUMA, the original aggregate music site.

IUMA, the Internet Underground Music Archive, was the original band site. They became a part of EMusic.com and got shut down, but were subsequently acquired and resurrected by Vitaminic, a European mega-band site. Their address remains http://www.iuma.com.

MP3.com (http://www.mp3.com) is the most well-known band site; they became a public company and got hit with lawsuits over their CD listening service. MP3.com is now a division of Vivendi-Universal.

Other sites that cater to indie bands include **Garageband Records** (http://www.garageband.com) and **GigAmerica** (http://www.gigamerica.com). All of these sites allow musicians to submit information, music and graphics. They provide a means to get on the Web in a quick and painless fashion. None of these sites require any HTML programming by the artist; page creation just takes a few copy/pastes and mouse clicks into their site-building forms. The sites mentioned here are free at this time — they don't charge musicians a penny for the service (although they may try to upsell you into "premium" packages.)

Note that these sites are also free to the listening public, meaning you're giving away your music by posting it there. Certain band sites have compensation schemes (more on that in Chapter 14) but for the most part band site participation is strictly a promotional effort.

Requirements

Before you begin uploading to band sites, locate and assemble the stuff you'll need, so you can be efficient while online.

Music - MP3 is the universal file format for band sites, and they all want stereo MP3s encoded at 128kbps. See Chapters 8 and 9 on preparing your audio and compressing it as MP3s. Make sure the music is your own, meaning both your own performance and an original composition. Cover versions aren't allowed at such sites (for now at least) because of licensing issues. Also, make sure it's a song you want to give away, because free downloads and streams are the deal here.

Graphics - Band logo, group photo, individual headshots, concert action pics, whatever you want to show. Most sites accept both GIF and JPG graphic formats; some sites have size restrictions so you may need to re-size or crop certain pictures for use on a particular page.

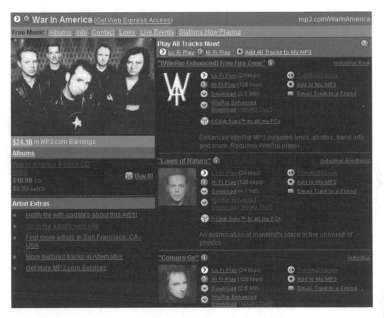

An example page from MP3.com, the 500-pound gorilla of band sites.

Lyrics - Have lyrics available in a word processor document or text file, so you can easily copy/paste them into the site-builder forms.

Bio - A few paragraphs about your act's sound, history or any other legend-building propaganda you wish to disseminate.

Song Descriptions - A couple sentences of "liner notes" for each song, perhaps noting prominent session players or providing some background for the listeners.

Band Member Info - At very least name and instrument.

Calendar Information - Dates, locations and times of upcoming performances or events.

Contact Information - Do you have a band e-mail address, Web site or other way for the public to reach you?

If you don't have all this stuff, don't worry. As long as you have one or more MP3 files you want to distribute, you're ready to hang a page — you can fill in any of the forms as you go, and you can always go back and update them later.

Uploading Your Materials

It will take 20 minutes or more to create your first page at a band site. If you're on a 56k dialup modem, figure on another 20 minutes or more for each song to upload.

When you first log into an "artist" area at a band site you'll have to establish an account, which will entail choosing a user name and password. You'll fill out one or more online forms with your contact information. The site will make you agree to the Terms Of Service; after you've accepted the Terms you'll hit a page that is used to select and submit your MP3 files, graphics and other information to the site. Certain sites offer some degree of customization, such as background or text color control.

It's all fairly self-evident, and you can generally skip non-critical parts (if you don't have a bio or lyrics, no big deal.) Some of these sites have an approval process; that means you must wait until a staff member listens to the track before it will appear on the public site.

At the end of the session you'll have a personalized Web page that anyone can view, and a URL that you can give to fans and friends so they can find your page. Band site URLs generally look something like:

Yet another band site example, this one from Angry Coffee (http://www.angrycoffee.com)

www.bandsite.com/BandName.html

If you want a more personalized and professional URL, such as **www.BandName.com**, you'll have to set up your own Web site. Read on to the next chapter to learn how!

11. Creating Your Own Web Site

The most powerful Internet promotional tool is your own Web site. Your site can create an impression of legitimacy that no aggregate band site page will ever confer. An effective, well-executed Web site is tangible evidence that you have your act together and demonstrates how well you promote yourself. It also allows you complete control over the impression your Internet visitors receive.

Creating your own Web page or Web site can be broken down into two parts: Writing the HTML code for your pages, and finding a home for your pages on a computer linked to the Internet.

And guess what: It's not that hard, thanks to the abundance of "drag-and-drop" programs that automatically create Web pages, and the increasing competition among firms offering cheap Web hosting.

About HTML

Hypertext Markup Language is a simple, text-based programming language that describes how Web pages should look and function. **HTML** lets Web browser programs know that the background of a particular Web page should be black, the text should be green, this picture should be here, etc. HTML also gives instructions regarding links and clickable objects (if the user clicks this button, send them here.)

HTML documents are nothing more than text documents, containing text, page formatting instructions and addresses (links) to graphics, audio files and other pages. HTML document names must have the file extension .HTM or .HTML in order to be displayed correctly by a Web browser.

If you've never seen what HTML code looks like, you can view and copy the code of any Web page you're browsing. Select the Source (or Document Source) command from the View menu of your browser. This lets you see how the author of the page made it look like it does. HTML documents are merely text, and you can actually write them in any ordinary word processor. But there are HTML editing programs out there that will make your job a lot easier.

HTML Editing Programs

HTML editors let you easily create Web pages in a WYSIWYG (pronounced wizzywig, short for What You See Is What You Get) environment. You simply type or paste in text, drag in graphics, and create links to other pages or downloads with a few mouse clicks. If you're looking for speed and ease of use, these programs are terrific. If you're not comfortable writing code, they're essential.

There are plenty of HTML editors to choose from, including such well-known programs as Netscape Composer (part of Netscape Communicator, distributed free,) Adobe GoLive (around $300) and Microsoft FrontPage (about $500.) Even the most expensive programs have demo versions or 30-day free trials.

You'll find a wealth of information on the Web and Usenet pertaining to Web site authoring, most of it free. There are also many books published on the intricacies of HTML code; when you're ready to try fancy stuff you'll probably benefit from owning one of them.

A screen shot from Microsoft FrontPage, an HTML editor for Windows.

Finding A Host

Before you put any pages up you need to find an online home for your Web site. Members of America Online get up to 12MB of storage space through the AOL Hometown program. AOL includes several built-in authoring tools that help automate the process of creating and uploading Web pages. They also have online tutorials and help.

Unfortunately, AOL has the right to censor any page if it contains "sexually explicit or otherwise offensive material." But if you're looking for a relatively inexpensive and user-friendly way of getting a Web site, you can't go wrong with AOL. You could start up an account with AOL at 5 p.m., and have e-mail and a Web page (albeit a very crude one) by 10 p.m., all for around $20 a month.

On the other hand, if you don't need all of AOL's adult-supervision and hand-holding, you can get much better hosting deals for even less money. Just making calls out of the Yellow Pages we were able to locate a local ISP offering 32MB of storage, plus dialup modem access and e-mail, for about $13 a month.

Broadband subscribers should remember that most Cable/DSL providers will throw in some number of Megabytes for a "personal Web space" as part of their basic service agreement.

Uploading Your Files

Your Web Hosting service or ISP will provide an FTP address, which is the place where your Web site files will reside on their host computer. FTP addresses look much like URLs (Web site addresses); for example:

ftp://ftp.serviceprovider.com/membername

You'll use an FTP client program to upload your Web page files, graphics and music to the FTP site. See the FTP section in Chapter 1; although most HTML editors now have FTP upload capabilities built-in, it's often very useful to have a stand-alone FTP client such as Fetch or FTP Voyager.

You'll need to remember your User Name and Password in order to gain access to your FTP site. Once connected you can upload your files and do any other maintenance like creating, renaming or deleting files and folders.

Basic Elements & Structure

Before you begin creating your own Web site, make a folder somewhere on your hard drive (or desktop) for storing the HTML documents that comprise your Web site. Give it a name like **myweb**.

Next, inside this "myweb" folder, create two subfolders: You can call them **images** and **music**, or other simple, single-word names. Here you will store the graphics and audio files that are part of your Web site.

Note that you don't want to build a Web site that links to graphics and documents scattered throughout your computer; such attempts are hard to upload and broken links may result. By the same token, you don't want to create a Web site where the HTML, graphics, music and other files are all mixed together in the same folder, because it's tough to manage.

Within your main ("myweb") folder you will have at the very least a home page. This page should be named **index.html** (or **index.htm**) so that Web browsers can identify it as the starting point for your site.

Other pages you create can be named whatever you want,

Web Surfing Tip:

Let's say you're trying to get to a site with the URL http://www.go.com/band/3, and you get an error message telling you that the document "does not exist on this server." Try backtracking a little and enter http://www.go.com/band or http://www.go.com and see if you can find it by going through the front door, so to speak.

An example of folder structure. HTML documents are on the "top" level, graphics and audio go in subfolders.

as long as they have .html or .htm at the end of the name, and as long as they are a single word, with no spaces. Any reference to an HTML document (or graphic or download) with a space in the file name such as web page.htm or band photo.gif can be misread by a Web browser, resulting in a broken link. Therefore make sure to use no-space names like webpage.htm or bandphoto.gif.

Although your Web site can be as unique and creative as you wish, many sites have similar elements worth considering when designing your own. Common features found on many artist Web sites include:

Home Page - The most common feature; all Web sites have a home page.

Music - Most artist Web sites have at least one central page, and frequently many sub-pages, from which music can be downloaded or streamed. Of course, you can provide links to music on your home page, or your can create separate pages for every album or song. And don't forget about the lyrics!

Bio - A description or history of the band, generally accompanied by photos.

News/Events - A place to advertise upcoming performances, record releases, etc.

Reviews - If people are reviewing your music at a band site or online magazine, you can link directly to the reviews. If you have print reviews from magazines or newspapers, you can post short excerpts (the best parts) without worrying about permission.

Links - You can link to anything on the Web. Typical links on a musician's Web site might include a record label, other bands, magazines, nightclubs, your own pages at aggregate band sites (like MP3.com) or links to other entities completely unrelated to music.

Commerce - Say you have a CD and t-shirts to sell. Or maybe you'd like to make a few bucks recommending other people's music. In either case you'll want a commerce page. Read on to Chapter 14, Selling Music Online, for details.

Photo Archives - A place to post all those rocking live shots.

Contact Information - How should people get in touch with you, in case they want to hand you a record deal? You may not want to put your home phone number on a Contact page because of privacy concerns; an e-mail address is generally considered sufficient.

Navigation

Once people find your home page, they'll need a way to get to the other pages on your site. The simplest way to help people tour your site is to create what's called a Navigation Bar, or **Nav Bar** for short.

Nav Bars typically appear along the top or left hand side of a web page. They offer links to other pages that are accessible from the current page. In a simple Web site, the Nav Bar might have links to all the other pages of the site, and the same Nav Bar would appear on each page of the site. In a complex site, each main page may have its own unique Nav Bar linking to its sub-pages.

A Nav Bar can be as simple as a line of text links: Home / Music / Bio / News and so forth. Note that text links generally appear as underlined in Web browsers, so visitors can see immediately that the text is a link. One would create the Nav Bar by typing out the names of the component pages, then highlighting and hyper-linking each word to its respective page. Next you can highlight the entire line of text, and copy/paste it into all the other pages of your site.

A much more fancy Nav Bar can be made out of graphic elements. Create a series of GIF or JPEG graphic "buttons," each of which contains a word or image that identifies one of your Web pages. Next, copy the buttons into your "images" folder. Then open up one of your Web pages in your HTML editor and import the graphics from the "images" folder into the page. Line up and arrange these buttons, either side-by-side or up-and-down, by dragging them around in the editor. Now click on each button to select it, then hyper-link the button to the appropriate Web page. Once you've linked them all you can highlight the whole group of buttons and copy/paste them into your other Web pages.

Two examples of Navigation Bars, both using graphic buttons.

An even more complex form of Navigation element is called a **Frame**. Frames can have traffic-trapping properties; pages at other linked sites will open up within the originating Frame. This behavior keeps your Navigation buttons visible in the browser window even as visitors travel to other sites. Frames had a real heyday a few years ago; today many Web designers and surfers find them intrusive.

Audio Downloads

The meat of any good music site is the audio. You can either let visitors download (and keep) your audio files for later listening, or you can stream audio, which is heard more or less immediately but is not retained by the end user. You may decide to offer both! We'll cover streaming audio in the next chapter; first let's discuss downloads.

Uncompressed audio files are far too big for Internet downloading, so you'll want to make copies of your songs in a compressed audio format such as MP3 or WMA; see Chapter 9, Compressed Audio, for instructions.

Some artists may be uncomfortable with giving away their work, and could elect to offer only brief excerpts of songs (like a 30-second preview) for downloading or streaming. That's cool, but know that most Internet music fans have been trained to expect complete songs; they might be disappointed by short segments.

At its most basic, linking to an audio file is no different from linking to a graphic. First drag or copy your audio files into your "music" folder. Next, type a line of text such as "Click Here To Download" within one of your Web pages. Then highlight the text and create a hyper-link to the audio file (located inside the "music" folder, right?). The HTML code for such a link would look like this:

<a href="music/SongTitle.mp3**">**Click Here To Download**</a>**

When a visitor clicks on this link, the file will be downloaded to their computer. When the download is complete the music can be heard with any compatible player. In some Web browser configurations (particularly those with QuickTime installed) this download link may instead open a new page and immediately play the file as a stream using an embedded player.

There are any number of other HTML commands you could incorporate which will affect the appearance and behavior of your download links. For example, you can display a custom message in the browser "status" area (along the bottom of the window) when the mouse is over a link:

<a href="music/SongTitle.mp3**" onMouseOver="window.status=**'This is a Custom Status Message**';return true">** Click Here To Download**</a>**

This is just one example; there are many, many other easy and cool things you can do with HTML. Take a peek at the Source of any sites you like, copy pieces of their code, and see what you can make!

DNS, short for Domain Name System, is how the Internet keeps track of addresses. Each Web site has its own numeric IP address, which looks something like 123.456.78.90. Humans do better with plain-language addresses, hence the advent of URLs (addresses such as http://www.mywebsite.com). The DNS associates URLs with their underlying IP addresses. When you move a Web site to a different server, or establish a new domain, your ISP or Registrar will need to update your DNS entry so visitors can find you.

Java and Other Web Site Goodies

Java is a programming language that lets Web site developers have fully operational programs that run inside the Web browser window. These programs are called "applets," and in their simplest form they can enable Web sites to have animation, like rotating logos or areas that change color every few seconds.

For more information about Java, and other free Web site building tools, check the Java section at Yahoo's Computers and Internet index.

Flash is a web animation technology that can be used to create cartoons, business graphics or even an entire Web site. Developed by Macromedia, Flash is ideal if you want an animated introduction or "front door" for your site, and many sites incorporate Flash throughout.

Most sites that implement Flash also maintain a non-Flash (standard HTML) version for visitors who don't have the Flash browser plug-in. Working with Flash is a discipline unto itself; drop by http://www.macromedia.com/software/flash to check out the authoring tools.

Most search engines and indices have an "Add URL" section that you can submit your site to. It may take several weeks or months to get listed on them, and you may have to submit your URL several times, but it's worth it. If no one knows about your Web site, it could become a "cobweb site."

"Under Construction"

Good Web sites, by their very nature, are continually changing and evolving. One used to see "Under Construction" notices on many Web sites, but that's gone away as people have begun to accept that most Web sites are perpetually under construction.

To keep visitors coming back to your site, be sure to change, add and refresh things on a regular basis. That doesn't have to mean a complete re-design every week, but bringing in some fresh news, a new track to download or photos from the last gig can help keep the cobwebs off your site.

As you're building and improving your site, it's advantageous to have both Netscape and Internet Explorer on your computer so you can check all changes in both browsers — they definitely vary in how they display certain things. If you can check your pages on both the Macintosh and Windows versions of IE and Netscape, better still.

If you're a broadband user, make sure to try browsing your site from a friend's 56k dialup connection. This will give you an idea of the typical page load time, and can be an important reality check, especially if your site contains many large graphics.

Your Own Domain

If you don't want your Web address to be something like http://www.small.town.isp.com/users/freebie/yourbandname.html, then you'll have to register, and pay for, a unique **domain** name. There's one important reason for registering your own domain: It's a heck of a lot easier to tell people to visit www.coolbandname.com.

InterNIC (now part of ICANN, the people who administer Web addresses) have a searchable database of Web domain names that are already taken at http://www.internic.net. When you find a name that's available, select a **Registrar** who can sell you the name. There are dozens of ICANN-approved Registrars; Arbor Domains (http://www.dirtcheapdomains.com) is one we happen to work with.

The Internet Corporation for Assigned Names and Numbers

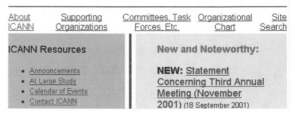

Home page of ICANN, the Internet administrative body that has taken over from InterNIC. http://www.icann.net

Once registered you can use your Registrar's DNS forwarding service to route Web visitors and e-mail from www.coolbandname.com to the actual server address where your Web pages reside. Alternately, your ISP may be able to provide the forwarding themselves, depending on your provider and your service agreement. Registering www.coolbandname.com should cost no more than $15 per year; this is a real "commodity" service so shop around for the best deals.

Having Someone Else Do It

If this all sounds like too much work there are a plethora of companies out there who will "Get You On the Web!" They range from cool people who happen to have access to the technology and are honestly into helping folks get online, to make-a-buck-quick types looking to cash in on Internet novices and unsuspecting musicians like yourself. As mentioned above, very inexpensive Web Hosting and design tools are available, requiring just a little research and work. So watch out for people who want to charge you thousands to get on the Web.

There happen to be a lot of people walking around with HTML, Flash and Java programming skills, many of them willing to help friends and acquaintances get their sites off the ground. Talk to people where you hang out — at work, at school, in church or in bars — eventually you'll run into folks with talents who can help you along.

12.Internet Radio and Streaming Audio

The quickest and most secure way to present songs to your Web audience is by using **streaming audio**. When you stream audio, the audio file is played for the listener as it downloads from the Web server to the user's computer. The listener does not retain a copy of the song on his or her hard drive; the audio is simply played and then discarded.

The advantage for the Web surfer is that streamed audio can be heard immediately, without waiting for the entire file to be downloaded. The advantage for the musician/webmaster is that the public can only listen to the music, they can't take it with them or share it with others.

One disadvantage to streaming is sound quality. In order for audio to be heard smoothly over a typical 56k modem connection it should be compressed to bit rates of 32 or even 24kbps. That means a significant compromise in sound quality, even when using the best-sounding formats. By comparison most downloadable MP3 files are 128kbps. (See Chapter 9.)

Another disadvantage is that Web surfers must have player software or a browser plug-in installed that supports the specific streaming format. They must also have their browsers configured correctly to recognize various streaming audio file types and to launch the appropriate player. Fortunately, Netscape and Internet Explorer come bundled with audio players and will generally set themselves up correctly during installation. Moreover, most Internet music players such as Music Match, Windows Media Player, or QuickTime will take over the rights to any supported streaming formats, by default, when they are installed.

It's really easy to offer basic, Do-It-Yourself streaming audio from your own Web site, or to set up your own station at one of the Internet Radio sites. We'll look closer at Internet Radio later in this chapter.

An MP3 or WMA file that is to be streamed should be small enough that it will play without interruption or delay on a 56k dialup connection. That means you'll want to compress such a file to a bit rate of 32kbps, 24kbps or even lower. Start with the original, CD-quality WAV, AIF or SD2 file — don't re-compress an MP3 or WMA — compressing already-encoded files causes an unnecessary reduction in sound quality.

Putting streaming audio on your site requires only slightly more expertise than posting regular audio files. If you've already posted a downloadable file on your Web site (as described previously in Chapter 11), then you're just one step away from adding a stream!

Streaming MP3: M3U

To stream an MP3 file you must create a "Metafile" called an **M3U**, which is an abbreviation of "MP3 URL." An M3U is simply a text file that contains a URL. This URL must be the location of the MP3 file that is to be streamed.

To make an M3U, open any word processor like SimpleText or Notepad and create a new document. This document should contain the complete URL of the file that is to be streamed, and would look something like:

http://www.serviceprovider.com/username/music/songtitle**.mp3**

That's all you need! Save the document with a file name that ends in the file extension .M3U, and for safety make sure there are no spaces in the file name.

Next, open any Web Page in your HTML editor and create some text that says something like "Click Here To Stream." Highlight the phrase to select it, then hyper-link the phrase to the new M3U document. The HTML code for this link should look much like this:

<a href="music/songtitle.m3u**">**Click Here To Stream**</a>**

Nullsoft SHOUTcast is a streaming MP3 system that lets you create your own personal radio channel. Now owned by AOL, you can get it at http://www.shoutcast.com.

Finally, connect by FTP to your Web server and upload your new Web page, the M3U "Metafile" you've just created, and the MP3 file it points to. Be sure to put the M3U and the MP3 in the right directory locations so that there are no broken links; in this example we're placing both the MP3 and the M3U into the "music" subfolder.

If all the links are okay your visitors should see their MP3 players open automatically and hear the audio immediately after they click on the link.

Streaming WMA: ASX

Streaming Windows Media Audio is a very similar process to the one just described. To stream a WMA file you first create a Metafile called an **ASX**. An ASX is just another text file that contains a URL. This URL happens to be the location of a WMA sound file.

Launch any word processor such as SimpleText or Notepad and create a new document. This document will contain a reference to the location of the WMA file, plus some additional tags, and must look something like this:

```
<ASX Version="3.0">
<ENTRY>
<REF href="http://www.serviceprovider.com/music/songname.wma"/>
</ENTRY>
</ASX>
```

Save this document with a file name that ends with the file extension .ASX (for example "songname.asx").

As before, open a Web page in your HTML editor, type in a line of text such as "Click Here for ASX Stream," then hyper-link that text to the intended location of your ASX file. Then upload your Web page, the ASX file and the WMA file to your Web server, each to its appropriate folder location.

Assuming your Web visitors have Windows Media Player (or another compatible player) installed on their PCs or Macs, and assuming their browsers are configured correctly, they'll see the player launch and then they'll hear the file being streamed to them.

RealAudio

Developed by Real Networks, **RealAudio** was the original and remains among the most popular streaming media formats on the Internet.

To do RealAudio you'll need a copy of the RealProducer encoder (also known as RealSystem Producer). RealProducer Basic is distributed free; the professional RealProducer Plus currently costs $199. Both RealProducer versions compress audio files into the RealMedia (.**RM**) format, and also create a metafile called a .**RAM** which points to the RM file (much like a M3U or ASX).

For basic Do-It-Yourself streaming, one would link to the RAM file from any Web page then upload the RM, RAM and HTML documents to the Web server.

Like ASX and M3U streaming, simple HTTP streaming of RealAudio from a Web server has a couple built-in disadvantages: First, you can only stream at one bit rate (kbps) per file; if you wish to offer support for different connection speeds you will need to encode a number of different files at vari-

One of the secrets to achieving better-quality sound with your streams is to use mono, instead of stereo compressed files. At 24kbps a stereo file would use 12kbps for each channel whereas a mono file will apply the entire 24kbps bandwidth to a single audio channel. Although the left/right image is lost, the overall sound of mono is mathematically twice as good as stereo at any given bit rate.

ous bit rates. Second, if you get a lot of traffic at your Web site and have many visitors listening to your audio at the same time, service may begin to deteriorate as each user takes some of the bandwidth at your server.

To address these limitations, RealNetworks offers server software called RealSystem Server and a technology called SureStream. A SureStream encoded file contains multiple copies of the audio encoded at various bit rates. RealSystem Server selects the appropriate bit rate according to the connection speed of each listener. This selection happens automatically so that each listener receives the best-quality transmission possible at whatever their current download speed.

Drop by http://www.real.com to download RealPlayer and RealProducer.

RealSystem Server also manages the traffic of visitors requesting your stream, removing that traffic load from your Web server. RealSystem Server is sold according to the number of simultaneous listeners it will support: RealSystem Server Basic allows up to 25 concurrent visitors and is offered with a free one-year trial period. RealSystem Server Plus can handle up to 60 users at the same time and currently costs around two thousand dollars. There is also a high-end option that starts at around eight grand.

All versions of RealSystem Server require Windows NT4 or 2000, Linux or the FreeBSD operating system; no Macintosh version is available at this time. RealSystem Server would be run on a computer at your ISP's hosting facility so talk with your ISP and make sure they can support this before embarking on a RealAudio development. RealNetworks also offers its own hosting and distribution services, but they are well out of the financial reach of the typical independent musician.

Live Webcasting

One of the most exciting things you can do with streaming is to present a live webcast. With the proper setup any concert or performance can be encoded as it happens and streamed to listeners around the world.

To do a live webcast, you'll need to be running either RealProducer or Windows Media Encoder on a computer at the performance venue. This encoding computer must be connected to the Internet by a high-speed line such as DSL or T-1. The encoder will be streaming the broadcast audio to a Web server or a dedicated RealSystem or Windows Media server at your ISP's hosting facility; this remote server will deliver the audio to your listeners.

When configuring the encoder you must set it up for broadcasting; in doing so you'll tell it where the broadcast should be sent to (for RealAudio) or drawn from (in the case of Windows Media): The name or IP address of the appropriate server; the port at the server where the broadcast will be transmitted (a four-digit number); and the file name on the server that users will access to hear the stream. You will have the option to Archive the broadcast, saving the compressed audio to a disk file for later listening.

Next, create a link on any Web page that points to the broadcast file name on the remote server, or send the URL as a link in an e-mail. Then connect the mixing board or microphones to the sound card input on the encoding computer, start the encoder software and begin your webcast.

Naturally there's a lot that can go wrong in this process: Simple audio cable failure, sound card problems, freezes or crashes by the encoder software, broken or misdirected links, incorrect port numbers, problems at the ISP's hosting facility or uncontrollable traffic slowdowns on the Internet — any of these issues can interrupt your broadcast. Be sure to test the system thoroughly before you go live "on the air" and allow plenty of time for debugging. Make sure that your ISP is aware of your broadcast and is able to support it.

After the broadcast remember to upload the new Archive file to your Web site, so that later visitors can hear the performance, even if they weren't able to catch it live.

Internet Radio Services

Internet Radio can be either live or pre-programmed. Many "terrestrial" radio stations stream their AM/FM programming live from their Web sites, thus giving their signals worldwide reach. Check out http://www.kzsu.org, the Stanford University radio station, or http://www.kfjc.org from neighboring Foothills College for two excellent examples of small local FM stations with world-class music programming.

A station list at Live365. http://www.live365.com

There are also a great number of pre-programmed or "on-demand" Internet Radio stations. Pre-programmed stations are generally a simple series of songs and ads. Some pre-programmed services, like AOL's **Spinner** (http://www.spinner.com) have corporate employees who make the music selections. Other services, notably **Live365** (http://www.live365.com) and AOL **SHOUTcast** (http://www.shoutcast.com) allow members of the general public to create their own personal Internet Radio stations.

Do-It-Yourself radio services are a terrific thing. You can create a program that heavily features your own music and music from your friends' bands and no programming director can stop you.

Live365's basic service allows members to upload MP3 files to Live365's servers. Members also upload a Playlist that specifies the sequence in which the MP3 files are to be played. Live365 adds the station to their listing and handles the streaming from their servers, repeating the Playlist continuously.

Live365 also offers a Live or "Relay" broadcast service, permitting you to do real-time programming. This option allows you to incorporate live DJing or turntable mixing as well as traditional radio production techniques including segues, announcements over music or live call-in spots. As with any live webcast, Relay broadcasting will require that you keep your computer on, and maintain a connection to Live365's server via the Internet.

If Do-It-Yourself radio proves impractical or just isn't your thing, another option is sending out CDs to already-functioning Internet broadcasters. Net versions of real-life radio stations are best approached offline, and you'll generally need to go through a gatekeeper such as the Programming Director or the Music Director. Some of the Internet-only stations are easier to approach. Many are fairly receptive to playing new music (some even concentrate on unknown bands) and most of them aren't formatted as strictly as AM/FM radio stations. There are a great number of genre-specific webcasts out there, so you should have no trouble finding stations that would be receptive to your style of music.

Content Delivery Networks

Content Delivery Networks, or **CDNs**, take care of the bandwidth and listener load issues associated with streaming media. CDNs can host audio files, live broadcasts or even entire Web sites through their networks of servers. CDNs operate networks of high-capacity servers and locate these servers at (or near) major entry points to the Net, positioning the machines at ISPs and Internet backbones.

Akamai is the best-known CDN and competes with such firms as iBeam and Digital Island. RealNetworks is also in the CDN business. If you expect hundreds or thousands of users to be hitting your Web site at the same time, consider using a CDN. Unfortunately, distributing through a CDN costs a lot of money and is beyond the reach of any indie band or small label.

A new generation of CDNs that utilize Peer-to-Peer hosting has recently cropped up. Companies such as AllCast (http://www.allcast.com) may eventually provide a viable lower-cost alternative to traditional CDNs like Akamai. Not sure what we mean by Peer-to-Peer? Then keep reading on to the next chapter, where we explain File Sharing!

13.File Sharing

If you are an artist releasing CDs on a major label (or a capable independent label) your music is very likely being given away on one of the Peer-to-Peer File Sharing networks right now. Some artists strenuously object to File Sharing and that's their right. Others see it as an opportunity, a way to reach the most-active music fans and get some exposure.

In an ideal world musicians would decide for themselves how to distribute their music. In the real world musicians frequently give their music away, are routinely ripped-off and even pay to play in some situations. File Sharing is here to stay. Love it or hate it, you should definitely understand it.

Basic Network File Sharing

File Sharing means letting other computers on a network access certain folders and files on your computer. File Sharing is built-in to every Mac and PC, just like printer sharing. One would use File Sharing in a business to allow co-workers on the office's Local Area Network to access documents on a hard drive.

To share any folder and its contents on a Windows PC, simply click on the folder with the right mouse button, select Properties, and in the resulting Properties dialog click on the Sharing tab. There you can turn Sharing on and off, control the type of access and establish a password if you so desire.

If you're on a Macintosh and want to share a folder with others, open the File Sharing control panel. This control panel lets you turn File Sharing on and off for your entire system. Next, mouse-click once on any folder you want to share and type Command - I (hold down the Apple key and the letter *i*). This opens the Get Info dialog for the folder. Click on the "Show" pop-up menu and select Sharing to view or adjust the sharing controls and privileges.

Once you've chosen to share a folder and its contents, other users on your Local Area Network or the Internet will be able to download and open those shared files. A computer that is sharing

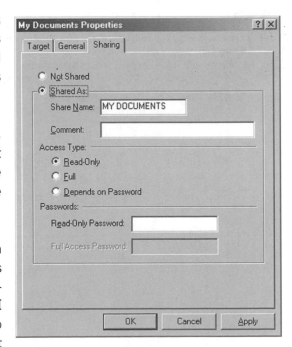

Windows users can turn on File Sharing in the Properties dialog for any folder. Click with the right mouse button to access Properties.

files is considered a **host** or **server**, a computer that takes files from that server is called a **client**. This arrangement is called a **client/server** network; it's very common.

Now if all computers on a certain network were both clients and servers, we'd call them "peers" and the network would be referred to as a **Peer-to-Peer** (or **P2P**) network. This was fairly humdrum stuff until a young person named Shawn Fanning came along.

Napster

Shawn Fanning's dorm mate was frustrated with the difficulty of obtaining MP3 files online, which at the time entailed trawling through Usenet or hunting down pirate Web pages. Fanning envisioned a way to let people easily share and trade their MP3 collections. Each user could be a server, sharing files that are in designated folders. Each user could also be a client, using a search tool to locate and download shared files from other people's computers.

Shawn Fanning's basketball court nickname "Napster" has become synonymous with Peer-to-Peer File Sharing. http://www.napster.com

The original **Napster** was a killer application. Fanning added Chat, so users could send messages to each other as they swapped files. There was also a "Hot List" feature that allowed one to view all the shared MP3 files on another user's computer, essentially snooping around people's hard drives to browse their music collections.

Music fans swarmed on board and Napster imitators began popping up. Napster started grabbing headlines and drawing heat from copyright owners.

Napster's "Music" folder, where it placed downloaded files on the user's hard drive, was shared with other users by default when the program was first installed. Thus any MP3 downloaded was automatically re-shared. The overall population of shared files increased each time a song was copied to another user's computer. In essence, Napster turned its users into music pirates from the moment the program was launched.

That's a powerful thing. We're talking about the instant criminalization of an entire class of people, estimated to number 50 million at Napster's peak. It drew into question certain aspects of ownership and control over recorded music, prompting a vigorous response from the music industry and eventually the U.S. Circuit Court.

Napster was not a "true" Peer-to-Peer networking system. It used central directory servers that maintained lists of computers currently on the network and the files they were sharing. Search responses came from these servers, which pointed to the actual files on the individual computers and directed download requests to those machines.

This "hybrid" arrangement utilizing central servers meant Napster could be easily unplugged. Some of the Napster imitators don't have this vulnerability.

Gnutella

Justin Frankel was the inventor of the Nullsoft Winamp MP3 player. He sold his company to AOL and had been working for his new corporate parent for less than a year.

In what was later described as an un-sanctioned outside project, Frankel and some teammates put together a Napster-style File Sharing program that did not require a central server. This program would establish and perpetuate a tree-like network, each user obtaining a small number of connections to other computers on the network. Search queries and results would be sent and returned across the network in a relay fashion, as every computer passed incoming messages to the handful of other computers it was directly connected to.

Such a setup is fairly difficult to shut down, since the network can exist and operate as long as the client application, or more specifically its networking **protocol**, is being run on two or more computers. Unfortunately, it's slower than the Napster arrangement; acquiring connections to other peers and receiving search results both involve some waiting.

A "protocol" is a method or language that allows computers to communicate with each other.

Frankel's program and the network it created were named **Gnutella** after the GNU Open Source License and a beloved processed food. The team posted the Gnutella application on an AOL Nullsoft Web page and issued an official-looking press release, resulting in a few thousand downloads.

AOL management soon figured out what was happening, tore down the Web page and rescinded the press release. But the program had already been posted to other Web sites and the undocumented Gnutella protocol was promptly reverse-engineered by a number of upstarts.

One of the big things about Gnutella and the programs that followed is that it's not just for music. Any and all types of files can be shared, including videos, graphics, text, spreadsheet documents, computer games and software programs.

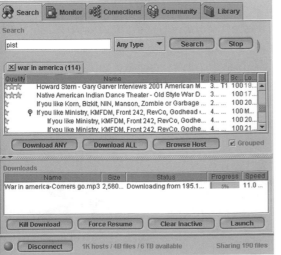

LimeWire, available for both Mac and Windows, is one of many File Sharing programs that use the Gnutella protocol.

The original Nullsoft Gnutella application is no longer in use, but many clone programs including BearShare (http://www.freepeers.com) and LimeWire (http://www.limewire.com) continue to support the Gnutella protocol and have advanced the functionality and feature set.

Among the key improvements is the use of "reflectors" to help users find connections to other users on the network. Reflectors maintain lists of computers currently on the network. New users logging onto the network can hit a reflector and receive referrals to other computers that are available for connection. Reflectors are a little like the Napster directory servers except they only provide an initial "jump-start" into the network, they don't maintain lists of hosted content.

Second-Generation File Sharing

In the wake of Napster a second wave of File Sharing networks have come on line. Some are managed networks that only deploy authorized, copy-protected files. Others are unmanaged networks and are typically awash with unauthorized MP3 files (plus porn and cracked software). There are many competing networks, and we mention here just a couple of the most prominent:

CenterSpan (http://www.centerspan.com) purchased the assets of Scour Exchange and re-launched the service as a legit subscription operation, based on a hybrid Peer-to-Peer setup similar in some respects to Napster. CenterSpan only distributes authorized content on their network.

Over on the pirate end of the spectrum you have **FastTrack** (http://www.fasttrack.nu), makers of **Morpheus** (http://www.musiccity.com). Instead of using a centralized directory server — which could be unplugged — Morpheus makes the users share the task of indexing content. The program first locates the best peers on the network, those with the fastest connections and most processing power. Dubbed "SuperNodes," the selected machines become search hubs. This allows Morpheus and other FastTrack programs to return quick search results from all the members of the network, yet remain decentralized.

Many individuals and businesses have shared folders on their computers, the kind described at the beginning of this chapter, and some of them may not even realize it. Shared folders are often not protected by passwords, and in many cases the computers are not behind Internet "Firewalls," a form of network security. As a result these folders could be accessible to anyone on the Internet who obtains your IP address.

ShareSniffer (http://www.sharesniffer.com) is a "shared resource indexing" application. Once installed, it enlists the user's computer in an ongoing project of guessing and trying IP addresses. When ShareSniffer discovers an

---

Don't worry excessively about picking up computer viruses or Trojan Horses from File Sharing networks. It's easy to avoid:
— Install any well-known anti-virus software package, set it up to scan your downloads (this is usually the default setting) and always have it running.
— Be cautious about downloading any strange file that ends with a .EXE file extension. Executable programs could easily be viruses or worms.
— You do not have to worry about picking up viruses from MP3, WMA, MPEG, AVI or other media files — there is no known way to attach hostile programs to audio or video files.

IP address that contains a shared folder, and determines that the folder is not password protected, it reports the address to a Usenet newsgroup.

ShareSniffer users can import these IP addresses from the newsgroup, snoop around any shared folder and copy the files within. ShareSniffer is a transgressive and somewhat troubling variant on the Peer-to-Peer idea. Whereas Napster made people into music pirates, ShareSniffer basically turns users into trespassers and burglars.

File Sharing Decisions

Is all this stuff legal? And should musicians participate, or try to shut it down? If you do not want your music shared and passed around freely by strangers you can hire Internet rent-a-cops such as **MediaForce** (http://www.mediaforce.com) and **NetPD** (http://www.netpd.com), the company that provided Metallica's evidence in their Napster lawsuit. These firms monitor the networks for offending content and help copyright owners notify ISPs or network operators that users are violating copyright law.

Fortunately, you don't have to enlist professionals to enforce your copyright. Many File Sharing programs display the IP addresses of the users who are hosting files, some even show the name of the ISP that is providing each host's connection. BearShare is a good example.

If you're a songwriter or copyright owner you have every right to download a File Sharing program, search out people who are pirating your music, then send letters and e-mails to the ISPs or network operators that are carrying unauthorized copies of your tunes. Be sure to include the specific IP address where your content was found, plus the exact time and date that the copyright violations occurred, in your notification letters. ISP reactions vary; some will pass along warnings to users urging them to tear down such materials, others might terminate accounts and force the bootleggers to move on.

On the other hand, maybe you're comfortable with sharing your music on Peer-to-Peer networks. There are a number of ways to increase your exposure and get new fans through File Sharing, and we'll show you how in the next section below. Before we move on, a quick ethics note:

It is wrong, all wrong, to distribute other people's stuff without their consent. We urge musicians to make use of any online resource, including File Sharing networks, to promote their music. And in the same breath we urge them and you, dear reader, not to share unauthorized tracks. Just offer your own music or licensed giveaway tracks. Download what you need — it's sometimes hard to know if a certain track is licensed or not — but only share stuff you know is okay to distribute. It'll keep you out of trouble and it's the right thing to do.

When radio began and broadcasters first tried to play records on the air, the result was an enormous battle for control over recorded music. It took more than a decade, a ton of litigating and a strike by ASCAP members to finally settle the issue. The battle for control of digital content sparked by MP3 and File Sharing may take just as long to resolve.

Increasing Your P2P Profile

If you decide that you will allow your music to be distributed over Peer-to-Peer (P2P) networks, you can sit back and wait for others to rip your CD and start sharing it, or you can get pro-active. The first thing is get your files together. If you skipped it before, have a look at Chapters 8 and 9 on digitizing, processing and encoding music for the Web.

Consider hosting both lo-fi and hi-fi versions of your files, offering people a choice of file sizes and bit rates. Although MP3 is the most popular audio file format for file sharing, consider encoding in WMA as well — and see the section in Chapter 15 on adding URLs to your songs — specially prepared WMA files can drive traffic to your Web site every time your song is played.

Remember to use the Tag features of your encoder to add information like Title, Author, Genre, Copyright, Description, etc. to the audio file metadata. The purpose here is twofold: First, Tag information can be displayed by audio player software, and utilizing Tags makes for a better listener experience. Second, Tags can be read by P2P search engines like Morpheus; good Tags get you additional hits. Some people really pack the Description field, adding tons of related words and even Spam terms like new, free, sexy and so on. See Chapter 9 for more on Tags.

Think about adding your band Web site's URL to the Tags for each song, and/or each file name, so new fans can find out more about you.

Next, make sure that each file name contains at least the name of your act and the name of the song. Audio files with names like **Track1.mp3** don't command much attention. If you're a little-known independent artist **Name of Band - Song Title.mp3** may not draw much traffic, either.

You can increase your exposure by adding a little star power. Perhaps you have a session player or band member who worked with a better-known act. Make a copy of the audio file and rename it something like **Name of Band - Song Title - featuring Better-Known Player formerly with Big Group.mp3**. That will get more hits, because now it's cropping up when people search for the "Big Group" or the "Better-Known Player."

The Morpheus File Sharing program can view and search Tag metadata. Note file description inset; fields such as Artist, Title, Album and Description are all coming from the Tag information. http://www.musiccity.com

Maybe you hired an accomplished producer, engineer or remixer — use the connection! Make a copy of the song and rename it **Name of Band - Song Title - Produced by Famous Producer, former member of Famous Act and producer of Band A, Band B and Band C.mp3**. That's a long name but now you can get hits from fans of all the artists mentioned.

Sometimes people look for music by region or style — you can have file names like **San Francisco California USA Powerful Uptempo American Alternative Industrial Dance Electronic Rock - Name of Band - Song Title.mp3**.

Another approach is to Spam your way into similar or unrelated bands' searches. For example, you can have a file named: **If you like The Beatles, Rolling Stones, Led Zeppelin, the Who, Dave Clark Five and Herman's Hermits download Artist Name - Song Title.mp3**. Hopefully the song in question would bear some resemblance to the artists mentioned. While fans occasionally take a chance on a track like this, such comparisons are less compelling than an actual star connection and usually draw fewer downloads.

In the end you should have a set of files, multiple copies of each song, possibly in different formats and sizes, with file names and Tags crafted to get exposure and hits when people are searching for words that relate to your work.

P2P Hosting Tips

Drop by CNET's Download.com at http://download.cnet.com and check the top downloads list to see which File Sharing applications are drawing the most users. You may wish to host on a couple of networks, alternating every day or so.

File Sharing programs need to know your connection speed (56k, Cable, DSL, etc.) so make sure to select the appropriate one during setup. To truly take part in P2P you **must** have broadband. A typical three-minute MP3 can be transferred in a couple minutes over Cable modem or DSL; it could take a half hour or more with a 56k modem.

These programs typically create a "Music" or "My Music" folder somewhere on your hard drive, and designate that folder as both the target for all downloads as well as the default Shared (upload) folder. This arrangement can generally be changed during installation, or at any time later by going into the Options or Preferences dialog. We recommend that users designate separate "upload" and "download" folders, and only share authorized music in the upload folder. All downloads (which may or may not be authorized) should go to a separate, non-shared folder. This way if you download questionable media you

Many ISP service contracts prohibit running servers on residential accounts. A File Sharing application is a type of server, therefore doing Peer-to-Peer hosting might violate the terms of service and put you at risk of getting disconnected. Bearing that in mind, when shopping for broadband talk to the ISPs in your area about running Napster-type programs. Alert them to the fact that you intend to share music. All of the customer service reps we have spoken to said it was cool and we wouldn't get hassled as long as we didn't share obviously pirated stuff like full-length movies or copies of Windows. ISPs basically just want your business.

don't automatically re-distribute it.

Check the Options or Preferences dialog for settings that determine the number of users, the number of uploads per user, bandwidth dedicated to uploads and related controls. You'll want to use the maximum allowable values, since you wish to provide the maximum number of uploads.

Gnutella network programs such as Bear Share or LimeWire allow users to turn off or ignore Incoming Searches or Incoming Hosts — you definitely do not want that if you are trying to host and distribute your own content. Make sure Incoming traffic is accepted, so that other users can locate your content.

TTL, short for Time To Live, controls the reach or duration of each search on the Gnutella network. TTL is measured in "hops," each hop being another computer that in turn relays the message to the next computer. If it weren't for TTL every Query would hop from computer to computer forever, and the network would quickly gridlock. Set the incoming TTL, the maximum time for searches from other computers, to the highest allowable value. That puts your songs within reach of the greatest number of computers.

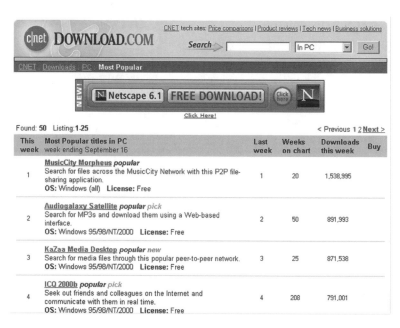

CNET's Download.com is a fantastic source of freeware and shareware, including all the latest File Sharing programs.
http://download.cnet.com

Some P2P File Sharing networks allow bands to register with the network in various ways. This usually takes the form of an "Artists" sign-up Web page, where the band or label representative would register their official consent allowing their music to be shared on the network. Some networks encourage bands to upload audio files, graphics and band information, creating an official group presence on the network or Web site. Certain networks require this kind of registration before allowing content to be traded, and will try to block or filter searches for unregistered (and presumably un-authorized) artist content. Naturally, you should make use of these sign-ups when present.

Now that your peer settings are optimized you can connect to a File Sharing network, let the program run day and night, and watch how many uploads you do. We've seen unknown bands give away as many as a hundred files a day using these type of techniques. That's a lot of traffic over the course of many weeks and months, far above what such a group might receive on their own Web site. Many of the people who take those files turn around and share their copies, thus increasing the overall population of the songs and making them even more available on the network.

14.Selling Music Online

If you're still with us after thirteen chapters of getting your music online, you may well be asking: "Can I make any money with this?"

The answer is **yes** there are easy (and not-so-easy) things you can do that make it possible to sell your music on the Web.

We'll mention examples of several specific companies and solutions in the course of this chapter; it bears repeating that commercial offers are subject to change without notice.

Band Site Payback

Some band sites have been willing to pay artists for their Web traffic or content. Although this business model seems to be losing favor there are still some noteworthy examples.

MP3.com's "Payback for Playback" system gives artists a "royalty" every time one of their songs is downloaded or streamed. If you are able to draw a lot of traffic to your MP3.com page, this can be a nice arrangement. Top bands are receiving several thousand dollars per month. It was originally a sponsored service; you'd just sign up and get paid. But MP3.com had to tighten up and now charges a monthly fee for participation in Payback for Playback. If you want to receive your "royalties," you have to pay in first.

MP3.com has a Statistics page where you can easily see how much Web traffic your page draws, the number of downloads and streams your visitors request and other information related to your page at MP3.com. It also shows how much Payback for Playback you might have earned, so you can determine whether it's a good investment to pay the sign-up fee and get your dollars.

MP3.com is not the only site with a payback system; Vitaminic's IUMA.com is still sending out quarterly artist royalties and other services are being launched that offer various compensation schemes.

D.A.M. CDs

MP3.com has another cool money maker, and this one doesn't require a buy-in: **D.A.M. CDs.** If you've already uploaded music to MP3.com, you're only one step away from making a D.A.M. CD and selling it over the net. MP3.com does all the legwork and the band can take the largest share of the money.

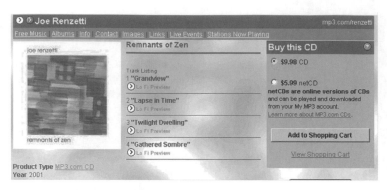

An MP3.com D.A.M. CD purchase page.

Just go into the Account Manager area and find the D.A.M. CD section. It already knows which songs you've uploaded, so simply select the tracks you want and place them in the proper order. Then you can upload cover art, liner notes, lyrics and so forth, as well as set a price and select a name for the CD. Done!

Once the art is approved, your CD will be available for sale. MP3.com sets up a purchase page linked to your artist page. They handle the purchase transactions, press the discs one-at-a-time and do a nice job printing, assembling, shrink-wrapping and shipping the CD. It only takes a couple days for U.S. purchasers to receive a D.A.M. CD, and it plays on any audio CD player and has a special multimedia player that launches when played on a computer.

The D.A.M. CD is a neat way to sell your music right now. Unfortunately, its sound quality is diminished by the fact that it relies on 128 kbps MP3 files as the audio source material — normally you'd never use a compressed file as the master for a CD.

Affiliate Programs

Affiliate Programs offer sales commission dollars in exchange for buyer referrals. If your Web site is a member of an Affiliate Program, you'll establish Web links to an online store, then get a cut of any money your visitors spend there.

To join an online retailer's Affiliate Program you first fill out an online form — they ask lot of questions because they'll be cutting checks to you — then you are assigned a **member ID** number. The member ID is used to track the visitors you'll send over. It's typically included in a special URL that you will use as the link to the retailer.

Affiliate Programs generally allow you great leeway in how you promote their products. If you just want to hang up banners or buttons, that's cool.

If you want to create your own "recommended reading" or "favorite music" pages, complete with custom reviews of each product, even better.

Amazon.com (http://www.amazon.com) runs one of the best-known Affiliate Programs and they sell a lot of books, videos and DVDs. Once you've signed up to be an Amazon "Associate" you can use their link-building tools to add buttons, search tools, banners or text links that point back to products at Amazon. Make sure to use their program-generated links which include your member ID number, and not the standard Web page URLs, or you won't get paid for your referrals!

CDNOW (http://www.cdnow.com), a division of Bertelsmann, runs a similar Affiliate Program called C2. Like Amazon they make you fill out a sign-up form, then have you use link-generating tools to create links to any CD, artist discography, label catalog or sales chart. As with the Amazon program, you're free to mention, recommend or outright advertise any of their products on your own site. If your Web site results in a sale, you get paid.

Although their commission percentages are relatively small, Amazon and CDNOW offer amazing selections. Both also have good report features, making it easy to see the amount of traffic, sales and commissions that your links are generating. Like all Affiliate Programs, the retailer does the heavy lifting of taking the sale, processing the transaction, fulfilling the order and sending you the check.

There are hundreds of other Affiliate Programs, often run by tiny firms with only one or two products. Some of them offer larger commission rates, up to 50% in certain cases. Many small software companies have adopted this sales method and there is a big concentration of Affiliate operations in the adult-oriented entertainment business. **ClickBank** (http://www.clickbank.com) is a good place to find reputable Affiliate programs.

In all cases your customers are purchasing from the online retailer, not from you, and you get paid only if the purchase is correctly referred to the retailer. If your member ID is missing or incorrect you will have blown it, so be careful when creating Affiliate links for your site.

Your Own Online Store

It used to be far too complicated and expensive for individuals to take credit card payments through their personal Web sites. To do real e-commerce one needed some heavy-duty CGI programming skills, a merchant account at a bank, a credit card push-button terminal and a trained monkey to key in all the numbers, sort the approvals from the declines and ship out the products.

Now you can run the whole thing through a simple Web service that handles the entire process except the final step. You'll still need that monkey to ship out the goods.

When you have your own online store you can sell any tangible physical product you want (such as CDs, t-shirts or posters) and you can determine the pricing, shipping and handling charges. You're on the hook for sending the orders and for any returns, but the online merchant service will provide the Shopping Cart, Secure Transaction processing and Invoicing in exchange for a small percentage of the transaction amount.

If you're going to build your own online store, make sure you understand the basic components. All e-commerce operations, great and small, have these features. Don't worry, you're only responsible for the first and last items!

Catalog - A Web page describing one or more products that are available for purchase.

Buy Link - A hyper-link in a Web page or Catalog, which connects the visitor to a Shopping Cart and adds the relevant item to the customer's list of purchases.

Shopping Cart - A Web page that represents the customer's list of intended purchases. It typically displays the name of the item(s), quantity and price, and has links that allow the user to return to the Catalog or to Checkout.

An example of a simple shopping cart.

Checkout - One or more Web pages in which the customer double-checks the purchase, selects shipping and handling options, and inputs their billing and shipping information.

Secure Credit Card Transaction - Sensitive sales information is encrypted by the Web browser as a security precaution before it is sent across the Internet, preventing eavesdroppers from intercepting Credit Card numbers and expiration dates.

Approval - Card number, expiration date and purchase amount are relayed to a server that checks the account and replies with either an authorization code or a decline message.

Invoicing - If everything's cool with the card, an Invoice is generated for the order and is e-mailed to both the customer and the shipping department.

Confirm Ship - Once the product has been shipped, a "confirm" message is sent back to both the Invoicing center and the customer, letting them know the process is complete.

It's easy to create a basic Catalog or Store page for your Web site; it can be simple lines of text, with maybe a few graphics. Once you have that, get with an online merchant service and look for one that doesn't charge any setup or maintenance fees.

We happened to go with **CCNow** (http://www.ccnow.com, not to be confused with CDNOW, mentioned above). The CCNow setup is quick, simple and suited to the needs of musicians. **PayPal** (http://www.paypal.com) is a comparable service that caters more to online auctioneers. Both will provide a simple Shopping Cart, handle all the checkout, transaction processing and Invoicing, and do it for a small percentage of the sale.

Once your account is established, the merchant service will provide Buy Links that you place on your Catalog page. These links drive purchasers to your new Shopping Cart and add the merchandise to the customer's purchase list. It's all pretty easy, and it took us a little more than an hour to create a simple Catalog Page, sign up with CCNow and hook up the Buy Links.

Some merchant services allow you to "co-brand" the Shopping Cart, providing room for a banner-style graphic. Most require that you place a graphic on your Catalog page identifying the service as your commerce partner. Both help reassure visitors that they're still within part of your site and buying from a known entity. The end result is a relatively seamless, professional-looking and very functional online store.

Selling Downloads and Streams

Services like CCNow and PayPal work great if you're selling physical product such as CDs or t-shirts. If you want to sell an electronic product — such as an audio stream, a downloaded music file or a software program — you'll need a system that handles the transaction and then permits the user to access the file.

As this book goes to press the situation is much like the old days of e-commerce: All of the pieces are available, but to put them together is too cumbersome and expensive for individuals right now.

The critical piece necessary for selling downloads is Digital Rights Management (**DRM**) technology, a fancy way of saying copy protection. When an audio or video file has been protected with DRM technology, only users who have a received a license (or **key**) can play the file. This key could be a password that is typed in, or a small data file placed on the hard drive that serves the same purpose.

THE MUSICIAN'S GUIDE TO THE INTERNET

In a simple DRM system, when a user first plays a protected file, the player software will attempt to contact a license server and retrieve the key. In most cases the user will need to give up their e-mail address or payment information to purchase the license. Once the key is received the file can be played on the user's computer.

There are a number of competing DRM systems. Most of them allow copyright owners to offer a "try-out" or "demo" period, to assign a variety of different usage rights and privileges, and to select a different price for each level of usage granted to the consumer.

InterTrust does a good job of explaining how its Digital Rights Management system operates; drop by http:// www.intertrust.com to learn more.

Once content has been encrypted and the content owners' "offers" have been applied, a license server and an e-commerce server must be set up. These systems will receive the key requests, harvest the required transaction information, process the sale if it's a credit card purchase and download the license key to the user.

To get this all going requires implementing one of the DRM SDKs (Software Development Kits) and that means you'll need to be a skilled programmer. Microsoft's Windows Media Rights Manager is the most prominent solution; InterTrust and Liquid Audio also have mature SDKs.

What we don't have available, although undoubtedly someone is working on it, is a simple turnkey service that does the file encryption, runs the license server and processes the transactions on behalf of lazy, cash-strapped musicians. Liquid Audio made an attempt at offering such a service some time ago, but it was subsequently scrapped.

Unlike downloads, to sell audio or video streams in a pay-per-view or subscription arrangement does not require any DRM technology per se. However, you'll need to put the stream links on a protected Web page and sell a password that allows purchasers to enter the page or view the link.

There are a few "electronic publishing" commerce solutions, notably **DigiBuy** (http://www.digibuy.com/), that can do credit card transactions resulting in a password exchange. Unfortunately, they're not really geared to the needs of musicians and don't want to handle small dollar amounts. Creating password-controlled Web pages on your site can also entail some fancy programming that is beyond the scope of this book. There is just no cheap-and-easy (or even just easy) solution, although we believe we'll see more options in this area in the near future.

Your Own Label

Now that you have an online store, why not set up your own record label?

If you have a CD-R/RW drive (a "burner") either built into your computer or as an add-on device, you can make up your own audio CDs and offer them for sale.

With some cheap color laser printing, available at any copy shop, plus press-apply disc labels such as the NEATO system, you can create reasonable-looking custom CDs of your music on a made-to-order basis.

If you want an even more professional presentation, things like silk-screen printing on the disc instead of press-apply labels, glossy insert printing or shrink-wrap, you'll need to go to a **replicator**. Discmakers (http://www.discmakers.com) is a well-known, full-service replicator, and they can handle all the CD pressing, printing and packaging. There are also many smaller competitors. By checking the Yellow Pages we were able to find a local service that would do runs as small as 100 copies for less than $5.00 per disc, including all the packaging.

The Discmakers web site is packed with information on how to prepare your music for CD release. Http://www.discmakers.com

Many musicians are offering both professionally manufactured CDs of their studio work as well as made-to-order CD-Rs of live performances and archive material. With the ease and widespread availability of home CD burning, there's no reason to keep recordings in the vault — offer them up for sale and make the discs as needed. It increases your label's catalog and allows you to recoup some money from those old gig tapes.

Naturally there is a lot more to running a record label than just hanging some Web pages, then burning some discs. There are many excellent books on the topic including ***Releasing an Independent Record*** by Gary Hustwit.

15.Building Web Traffic

Once you have a cool Web site, an online store or even just a page at a band site, you ought to promote it in order to get people to visit, listen and spend money. Promotion is an art and profession unto itself and we couldn't possibly cover all the angles here, but we will touch on some of the key things that any musician/Webmaster should consider.

Measuring Web Traffic

Before you start hyping your site, make sure you can measure the effectiveness of your efforts. The practice of collecting statistics about Web traffic is called **Metrics** or **Reporting**.

Band sites such as MP3.com have built-in Report features; once you've logged into the account management area you can check out graphs and other information on the visitors and listeners your pages have drawn.

For your own site you should hook up an audience measurement mechanism. Odometer-style page-view counters were once a common feature on homespun Web sites. One still occasionally sees these: "You are visitor number 0000039 since January 1, 1994." This type of meter that is visible to the public is now considered hopelessly gauche.

You don't necessarily want your visitors to know how many (or few) views your page is receiving. And you could benefit from getting more detailed information about your visitors: Where do they come from? What kind of systems do they use? What do they do while at your site?

There are a number of services that provide detailed Web site statistics free of charge. Once you've signed up with one of these operations, such as **MyHitLogger** (http://www.myhitlogger.com), you'll receive a block of HTML code. The code is simply pasted into the body of each Web page (you'll need to be viewing and editing the Source HTML for this) and typically goes near the bottom. Make sure you add this tracking code to every page in your site or you'll get an incomplete picture of your actual traffic.

When you've uploaded your modified pages you'll see a new button or graphic from the statistics service on each page. These graphics function as hyper-links back to the Metrics firm and also serve as evidence that the tracking code is in place on the page.

We've settled on **WebTrends Live** (http://www.webtrendslive.com) for both corporate and personal Web sites. WebTrends has a simple sign-up and setup, and it should take you an hour or less to open your account, add the WebTrends Live HTML code to your pages and upload them to your site.

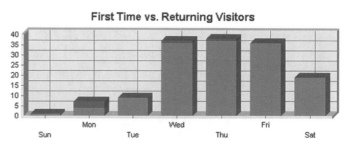

Check your stats at least every week or so and you'll be able to learn a great deal about your audience. Want to see first-time viewers compared to returning visitors? No problem. How many of them are on Macintoshes or use Netscape? Are people viewing your site from businesses, schools or maybe the government? What links are they following to reach you? All this and more can be shown quickly and easily in colorful charts and diagrams.

One of the many types of reports you can view about your Web site traffic. This example is from WebTrends Live (http://www.webtrendslive.com).

Bookmarks and Home Pages

Every Web browser has **Bookmarks**, called **Favorites** in Internet Explorer, which save the address of any Web page so it can be easily returned to later. To Bookmark the page you're currently viewing on a Mac, press Command-D (that's Apple key and the letter *d*). On a PC, press Control-D.

Every Web browser also has a **Home Page** — or more precisely, a default start-up page that is viewed each time the browser is launched. To change the Home Page in Internet Explorer, select Internet Options from the Tools menu and enter the new Web address (http://www.whatever.com) into the Home Page field. In Netscape Navigator, select Preferences from the Edit menu, then under the Navigator category enter the new URL and click on the "Navigator Starts With Home Page" radio button.

Because these features are so prosaic, they are often overlooked; there is tremendous promotional value in getting people to make you their Home page or a favored Bookmark. Urge your true fans to make your cool site their Home page. Keep the site fresh and constantly changing so it's a rewarding experience for them.

HTML Meta Tags

An HTML document can contain special labeling information that will help Search Engines categorize the Web page. These labels are called **Meta**

Tags and they're not too different from the Tags one adds to an MP3 file (see Chapter 9). Meta Tags are visible to the robots that are used to compile Search Engines, are shown in Search result listings, and help determine your page's ranking in any Search result.

The three most important Meta Tags for Web pages are Title, Keywords and Description.

To create these Tags simply open up any of your Web pages in an HTML editor (or word processor) and view the Source code. This is one of the few places mentioned in this book where you must write some HTML code; fortunately, it's easy and you can copy the example below. Meta Tags are positioned at the beginning of the document between the Head tags. When completed, your Meta Tags should look something like this:

<head>
<title>Home Page of This Cool Band **</title>**
<meta name="keywords" content="Name of Band, Member1, Member2, Member3, Musical Style, Location, Associated Artist, Music, MP3, Other Keywords**">**
<meta name="description" content="Home Page of This Cool Band from California Featuring Free MP3 Music**">**
</head>

Title should be a brief, one-phrase description of the Web page, 40 characters or fewer. Just a couple of words will do. The Title is displayed by most Web browsers, visible in the Title Bar at the top of the browser window. The Title must appear right after the <head> tag. Putting the Title anywhere else in the HTML document will hide it from some Search Engines. Do not use any word in your Title more than twice and don't use all CAPS.

Keywords are important words or phrases that relate to the content on the Web page. Your band name, member names, label, musical styles, associated artists and venues are all potential Keywords. Select Keywords that you wish to be found and ranked under. Keep the Keywords tag 874 characters or fewer and list Keywords in the general order of their importance. Although it's okay to repeat Keywords, do not put them next to each other and don't use any Keyword more than three times.

WEB RESULTS
1. Cajun/Zydeco **Music** and Dance – A large collection of links related to **Cajun** and Zydeco **music**, dance, and culture.
Arts>Music>Styles>World> **Zydeco**
[Translate]

2. Gary Hayman's ZydE-Magic **Cajun**/Zydeco **Music** & Dance Site – Extensive source for **Cajun** & Zydeco **music** and dance information including articles, schedules, photos, **music**, band and regional organization information.
Arts>Music>Styles>World> **Zydeco**
[Translate]

3. Cajun French **Music** Association – The **Cajun** French **Music** Association is a non-profit organization dedicated to the promotion and preservation of **cajun music** and culture.
Regional>North America>United States>Louisiana>Arts and Entertainment>Music> **Cajun**
[Translate]

Meta Tag information is used to create Search result listings. Note the use of the Title and Description tags in this example from Lycos (http://www.lycos.com).

The **Description** is a one-sentence summary that serves as the sales pitch for your page. You have around 25 words or fewer to attract any Web surfer who may have found your site in a Search. Keep your Description under 150 characters. Description and Title are the fields most likely to be displayed in a Search result, so make sure they convey what your site is all about.

There are a number of free Web page analyzers, such as the one offered by **Scrub The Web** (http://www.scrubtheweb.com), that will examine any Web page then suggest changes that can improve its Search Engine rankings.

Submitting to Search Engines and Fan Sites

The point of the whole Meta Tag exercise is that you're going to submit your site to Search Engines. Many Search Engines use robots that spider across the Web, cataloging each link so that new sites can be included in their index. For the robots to find your site, you must sign up. Each Search Engine has a link for adding new URLs, typically buried near the bottom of the page. Be diligent about submitting each of your Web site pages to the major Search Engines, then be patient because it can take weeks or even months for the robots to get around to crawling your site and adding it to their indexes.

There are a lot of Search Engines, and because they wax and wane in popularity you should submit to the major ones first. Here's a short list in approximate order of priority:

Google (http://www.google.com)
Yahoo! (http://www.yahoo.com)
Search.MSN (http://search.msn.com)
AltaVista (http://www.altavista.com)
Lycos (http://www.lycos.com)
Excite (http://www.excite.com)
AskJeeves (http://www.ask.com)
Mining Co./About (http://www.about.com)
GoTo (http://www.goto.com)
Netscape Directory (http://search.netscape.com)
Dogpile (http://www.dogpile.com)
Go2Net (http://www.go2net.com)

There are a number of Search Engine submission tools that try to automate the process to varying degrees and will submit your site to any number of Engines. These can be a good way to quickly pick up some additional listings as long as the submission tool is free. You shouldn't pay for such a service — you should do it yourself for the top sites.

Unlike some other Search Engines, Yahoo uses actual human beings to

If you have a CD that is being distributed, submit your CD information to CDDB (http://www.cddb.com). This online database is used by most player/encoder software to provide artist, title, track name and other information when playing or ripping CDs. Just connect to the Internet, launch MusicMatch or any other major player software and insert your disc in the computer's CD drive. If there's no match in the database, you'll be asked if you want to add a new CD. CDDB enhances the user experience and ensures your name is spelled correctly when your CD gets ripped.

do much of the cataloging. Every new site must be submitted for a particular section of Yahoo, and its categories go pretty deep. For instance, if you're in a Latin Jazz group you might want to submit to Entertainment > Music > Artists > By Genre > Latin > Latin Jazz. Submit pages one time each to all of the best Yahoo categories, then sit tight. Yahoo's in no rush to consider your page unless you've signed up for their Express service, which costs a couple hundred bucks.

Yahoo and many other Search Engines still allow free submissions, but some Search Engines require fees. A small business might consider shelling out a few hundred dollars for a Search Engine listing but it's not a reasonable investment for most musicians. You'd be better off getting links from Web sites that cater to your style of music or your regional music scene.

Fan sites can be incredibly specialized. This page is from a site devoted to the Welsh Pop scene at http://welcome.to/welshpop

Whether you play Jazz, Rock, Electronic or Polka, there are online music magazines, band directories and fan sites devoted to your form of music. Typically run by music lovers, most would be happy to review your CD, add a link to your site or perhaps feature your act if they dig your music. You can find these sites by poking around the Music Genres section of Yahoo or any other major index. Look for the contact information on sites you like, because they often publish submission guidelines. There are also Web sites that cater to particular cities or regions and many of them have event calendars or will accept listings from local artists and performers.

Expect to spend several long sessions doing your first round of submission work. One evening should be adequate to cover the major Search Engines, then spend some time digging up grass-roots sites that focus on your type of music. Don't forget to follow up by sending out CDs; most webzines won't review a Web site. Remember that promotion is a never-ending process and you should always be doing things that will draw traffic to your site and attention to your music.

Mass Mailings

To get a mailing list started, first pool the address books of each of your band members. The easiest way to do this (if you're not all running the same e-mail program) is to have them Export their address books as comma delimited text files. For simplicity they should just Export the e-mail address fields; that's all you really need. Once you have the e-mail addresses you can import them into a spreadsheet or database or just copy them into a word processor document.

Next, set up a mailing list link at your Web site so you can harvest new addresses. You might want to add this link to your Home page or any other high-traffic parts of your site. First, open the Web page in your HTML editing program, and then create a line of text that says something like: "Click Here to Join Our Mailing List." Next, highlight the text and create a hyperlink to an e-mail address; it should look like this:

<a href="mailto:list@mybandsite.com**">** Click Here to Join Our Mailing List **</a>**

The **mailto:** must be followed by the e-mail address that will receive the requests, with no spaces after the colon. When a visitor clicks on this link their e-mail program will open a new pre-addressed message. One way to increase sign-ups is to run a promotion — one might offer to give away CDs or t-shirts to new list members selected at random.

Most professional e-mail programs will let you create an auto-reply message, so that you can respond to people instantly with a standard thank you letter when they join your list.

Copy the new list members into your master list, spreadsheet or database before each mailing. Remember to use the **BCC** (Blind Carbon Copy) address field for all your mailings, so people aren't forced to read (and can't copy) your entire list of recipients. See Chapter 4 for more e-mail tips.

No matter what the purpose of your e-mail, make sure that your Web site URL is somewhere in the message. Most people who receive an invitation to a live performance don't show up for some reason, but nearly all of them can click on a link in your e-mail message and check out your site or band page.

Another tactic to consider is adding your Web site URL to your e-mail **Signature** so that it appears in every e-mail you send. Signatures are standard lines of text that are added to the bottom of each e-mail message. They typically contain your name and contact information, and often feature a witty saying or proverb; they should always include your Web site address. Nearly any e-mail program will let you set up one or more Signatures.

Because people are sensitive about Spam, add some type of disclaimer and opt-out instructions at the bottom of all mass mailing list messages. This disclaimer should say something like: "You are on My Cool Band's mailing list. If you were added to this list in error or no longer wish to receive these messages, send an e-mail to drop@mybandsite.com and you will be removed from future mailings." Try to be diligent about promptly and completely removing people from mailing lists when they ask to be dropped. Some sensitive individuals will actually notify ISPs about persistent Spammers; we've seen accounts blocked as a result of such complaints.

Link Exchanges

Having lots of links to your site from other people's Web sites makes it possible for new visitors to find you and thus improves your rankings in Search Engines. You probably know other musicians with their own Web sites. Offer to add them to your Links page if they'll make a link to your site.

If you record at a professional studio, practice at a rehearsal facility, use an instrument repair shop or gig at a nightclub or social center, chances are those companies also have Web pages. When you're spending money or doing work that supports their business, you have solid leverage to persuade them to add a link to your site. Many firms routinely put client rosters online, so just ask to be added. Offering a link in exchange will usually seal the deal.

Earlier we mentioned other online participants, such as fanzines, genre sites and band directories, all of which you should seek out and contact as you attempt to promote your site.

Web Rings are a variation on Link Exchanges in which a group of similar or affiliated sites agree to share traffic between the member sites. Each site adds a link to the bottom of their pages that directs users to the next site in the Ring. Web Rings were a semi-hot thing a few years ago but you don't see them much anymore and their traffic-building value is thought to be limited.

Adding URLs to Your Songs

If you give away music through your Web site or share your songs on a Peer-to-Peer network, you can enhance those audio files so that they drive listeners to your Web site every time they are played. This is a powerful promotional tactic that allows you to display lyrics, artwork, band information and yes, even advertising to listeners as they enjoy your music.

Back in Chapter 9 we mentioned that compressed audio files can contain Metadata. Essentially bits of text added to the file header, Metadata has no impact on the audio sound quality and adds very little to the file size. The most common forms of audio Metadata are Tags, such as the ID3 Tags found in MP3s.

URL scripts are a more specialized type of Metadata. When a URL script is inserted into an audio file, the player software will execute the script, launching a Web browser and opening the specified Web address each time the file is played.

WMA is the best format if you want to use URL scripts. Just download **Windows Media Encoder** to your PC (sorry, no Mac version) and create a new encoding Session and a new Profile that include Scripts as an input Source. Then you'll encode your WAV file into a WMA. Type or copy/paste the URLs into the Script panel as the file is encoded. It's not the most intuitive process but it's easily mastered and it really works. Anybody with Windows Media Player and an Internet connection will see your Web pages pop-up each time he or she plays the file.

URL scripts can be inserted into MP3 files, but this is not part of the standard MP3 specification and most MP3 players won't recognize the Metadata. Download a trial copy of InterVideo's **WinRip Studio** encoder (http://www.intervideo.com) if you want to play around with URLs in MP3s. WinRip Studio has a slick interface for adding lyrics and URLs. Inserted information will be displayed if the listener uses the WinRip player. Sadly, WinRip is only available for Windows.

Windows Media Encoder lets you insert Web page addresses into audio and video files. Note the Script Panel in the lower section of the screen — this is where URLs can be typed or pasted in while encoding. Download a free copy at http://www.microsoft.com.

In either case you'll create a file that can be downloaded or steamed just like any other WMA or MP3. When the recipient listens to the file their Web browser will open and they will be shown the Web page(s) you have specified. This little-known technique is one of the most direct ways to generate music-oriented Web traffic. It converts files you give away into measurable audience numbers, additional promotional exposures and new sales opportunities.

Offline Promotion

Your Web site URL should be printed on everything you own. Put it on stickers, letterhead, business cards, fliers, postcards, t-shirts, catalogs, tapes, CDs, promo photos and anything that you sell or give away. All ads you take out, whether in local music rags promoting a show or in national mags promoting a release, should include your URL.

It's now very normal for artists to mention their Web address from onstage, directing audience members to check out the site later on. If you perform with a backdrop or a light show, you might even consider working your URL in there somehow. Naturally you should be talking up your Web site and your band to everyone you encounter.

You can get many useful promotional ideas just by looking at other online and offline businesses. There is a wealth of information about promotion techniques available at the local library; *The Guerrilla Marketing Handbook* by Levinson and Godin is one fine example.

16. Conclusion

Hopefully you now have a better idea of what the Internet is and how it can help your music career.

We hope this book has helped you establish some sort of presence on the Internet. E-mail is a must-have; it's so easy and pervasive that anyone can advantage of it. We think it's crucial for you as a musician to get a Web site, any Web site, up on the Net as soon as possible, even if it means just hanging a page at one of the mega-band sites. A picture and some info about you or your band is good enough for starters and it's important not to stop there.

Once you have a temporary site online, begin working on the "real" site featuring more audio, graphics and writing that will attract and retain new visitors and fans of your music. As you learn about Web site construction, you can add more and more features to your site. If you get stuck on a technical problem, try doing a little research — the Net was made for that — or ask a friend.

We think musicians should take a stab at trying to earn some money online with their music. More and more artists, famous and obscure, are making it pay and you can too. We also think you should consider giving away some of your music, either at your Web site or on one of the Peer-to-Peer File Sharing Networks. It's good exposure and if you're pro-active about it you can make it pay off in other ways.

Experience is the best teacher. No book can take the place of actual online time, so the sooner you're surfing the Net, the better. Just by exploring and doing stuff you'll pick up tips on how to use the Internet to your best advantage. The first priority is to get a decent computer and browser program. Then get out there.

Now Go Wild,

Todd Souvignier & Gary Hustwit

Appendix: Glossary

. - This is not a period. On the Internet, this is a "dot." When you tell someone an e-mail address (joe2001@aol.com), it's "joe 2001 at A-O-L dot com."

AIFF (or .aif) - A Macintosh audio file format.

affiliate - A Web site that refers customers to an online retailer in exchange for a sales commission.

alt - Usenet newsgroups devoted to "alternative" topics, like alt.tequila and alt.music.ramones.

America Online (or AOL) - A commercial Online Service.

ASCII - American Standard Code for Information Interchange. ASCII is a standard computer character set used by most computer systems worldwide. An ASCII file is a text-only file.

ASX - A streaming Windows Media Audio metafile.

attachment - A data file that can be added to, and sent with an e-mail message. Such files could be text documents, pictures, sounds, etc.

AU - An audio format for Unix computers.

AVI - A Windows video format.

band site - Refers to aggregate Web sites such as IUMA or MP3.com that host pages from hundreds or thousands of different artists. Used here to distinguish it from one's own Web site.

bandwidth - The amount of digital data that can be sent through a connection such as a phone line or cable.

BBS - A bulletin board system. A computer system running bulletin board software that allows users to phone in, access discussion groups, and send mail. These systems are sometimes attached to the Internet.

BCC - Blind carbon copy. An e-mail addressing option used when sending e-mail messages to a large group of people, so that the recipients won't be able to see who else received the message.

BinHex - A way to encode data files so that they can be sent over the Internet. A form of file compression.

Bit Rate - The data bandwidth requirement of a compressed audio file, measured in kbps. Indicates the general sound quality level of the file.

Bookmark - A way that you can remember your favorite places on the Internet with your Web browser. Called "Favorites" in Microsoft Internet Explorer.

bps - Bits per second. This is how modem speed is measured (e.g., 56,000 bps). See also kbps and Mbps.

broadband - Any Internet connection faster than a 56k dial-up modem. Generally refers to Cable modem, DSL or faster services.

browse - The act of viewing and using resources on the Internet.

browser - A program used to view sites on the World Wide Web. Netscape Navigator and Microsoft Internet Explorer are browsers.

burner - A CD recorder. Also called a CD-R/RW drive (see below).

buy link - A hyper-link on a Web page that connects the visitor to an e-commerce Shopping Cart.

Cable modem - A form of broadband Internet service offered by cable TV operators that utilizes a coaxial cable.

CDN - Content Delivery Network. Used for high-traffic Web sites and streaming operations; Akamai is a CDN.

CD-R/RW drive - Compact Disc Recordable/Re-Writeable drive. A device that will record CDs containing music, data files or both.

chat - Passing written messages with someone in real time over the Internet.

checkout - Web pages used to complete an e-commerce transaction.

client - A computer or program that is requesting files from a server.

codec - Short for compression/decompression. A program or process that reduces the size of a file. MP3 and WMA are audio codecs.

compression - Decreasing a file's size so that it can be more easily transferred over the Internet. MP3, WMA and RealAudio are all audio compression schemes.

CompuServe - An Online Service, now part of AOL.

cyberspace - A term some people use for the "place" you are at when you're online. Popularized by writer William Gibson.

dial-up - An Internet connection over telephone lines using a 56k (or slower) modem. As opposed to "broadband."

Digital Rights Management - Also called DRM, this is copy protection for audio, video or other types of digital files. Typically involves a password or key which grants the usage rights that have been licensed to the consumer.

discussion groups - Any "place" on the Internet where discussions are held, including mailing lists and Usenet newsgroups.

DNS - Domain Name System. The system that translates between the natural-language URL Internet addresses and the numeric IP addresses.

domains - The different parts of a World Wide Web URL. The Top Level Domain designates whether the host computer is a business (.com), a school (.edu), a non-profit organization (.org), a branch of the government (.gov), etc. The Second Level domain is the name of the host computer (aol.com) and must be assigned by a Registrar. Third Level domains are sub-servers (mail.msn.com) and may be assigned by the domain owner.

download - To transfer a file from another computer to your computer via the Internet.

DRM - Digital Rights Management (see above).

DSL - Digital Subscriber Line, a form of broadband Internet service that utilizes phone wires or a wireless connection.

e-commerce - Selling things over the Internet. Often refers specifically to taking credit card numbers through Web pages.

e-mail - Electronic mail.

emoticons - Those little sideways smiley faces some people on the Internet use to show emotions :-)

encoder - Software used to create a compressed audio or video file.

encryption - A way to protect a file or e-mail message so that only the intended recipient (who has the correct decoding software, or "key") can read it. Digital Rights Management relies on encryption.

Eudora - A popular e-mail program.

FAQ - Frequently Asked Questions. These are files on Web sites and newsgroups which list the frequent questions about the site and give the answers.

file sharing - Allows other users on a network to download certain files from your computer. A feature of all computer operating systems. Napster was the most famous music file sharing program.

flame - An insulting or angry e-mail message or Usenet posting.

Flash - An Internet animation technology developed by Macromedia.

freeware - Free software available on the Internet.

FTP - File Transfer Protocol. The Internet method of transferring files from one computer to another.

GIF - Graphics Interchange Format. A type of compressed graphics file (picture) commonly used on Web pages. GIF file names will end with .gif.

Gnutella - A Peer-to-Peer File Sharing protocol and network developed by AOL's rogue Nullsoft division. BearShare and LimeWire are Gnutella client programs.

hang - Slang for uploading files to a Web site.

home page - The main page or "front door" of a Web site. Also refers to the default start-up page in a Web browser.

host - A computer linked to the Internet that "hosts" Web sites or other resources. Also known as a server.

HTML - Hypertext Markup Language. The language that is used to write Web pages. Browser programs read HTML and translate it for your computer.

hypertex - Text that contains links to other documents.

ICQ - An Instant Messaging application, now owned by AOL.

ID3 - A type of metadata used to provide labeling for MP3 files. There are two flavors of ID3 tag, ID3v1 and the more comprehensive ID3v2.

Instant Messaging - A type of private, real-time online chat. Similar to e-mail in that it is done with people in a personal contacts list.

Internet - The global network of computers.

Internet Explorer - A Web browser program made by Microsoft.

IP Address - The numeric address of a computer on the Internet.

ISDN - The original "broadband" modem service.

ISP - Internet Service Provider. A company that offers access to the Internet, but usually does not provide proprietary content or services, as distinguished from an Online Service.

IRC - Internet Relay Chat. A protocol and program that lets you chat with people in real-time on the Internet.

Java - A programming language that allows you to run special programs within the Web browser window, initially developed at Sun.

JPEG - Another compressed image file format, often used in Web pages. JPEG file names have the extension .jpg.

key - Used with encryption or Digital Rights Management systems to unlock a protected file.

kps - A measurement of modem speed, in kilobits per second (e.g., 56kps), also written as kbps (see below).

kbps - Kilobits (thousands of bits) Per Second. A measurement of transmission speed or bandwidth requirement. Refers to modem performance (e.g., 56kpbs) and is also used to indicate the general sound quality level in a compressed audio file (e.g., 128kbps).

link - A highlighted graphic or selected text on a Web page that will take you to another part of the Web site, or to a different Web site, if you click on it.

log in (or **log on**) - To start a session on your Internet account.

M3U - A streaming MP3 metafile.

mailing list - A group of people with a common interest who all receive the e-mail sent to the list.

Mbps - Megabits (millions of bits) Per Second. An indicator of transmission speed, generally used when referring to higher-speed broadband service (e.g., 1.5Mbps).

Merchant Account - A business account at a commercial bank that is used to receive credit card payments.

metadata - Text information added to the header portion of a compressed audio file that helps describe the file. ID3 Tags are examples of metadata.

metafile - A file that points to or describes another file on the Internet. ASX and M3U are both metafile types.

meta tag - HTML coding statements that describe the contents of a Web page and are added to improve its visibility and placement within Search Engines.

metrics - Statistics concerning traffic and activity at a Web site.

MIDI - Musical Instrument Digital Interface. A system that lets synthesizers, drum machines and other musical devices share performance data. Commonly used in electronic music production.

modem - A device that connects your computer to the phone line (or cable) and to the Internet or another computer. Short for "modulator/demodulator."

mono - Short for monophonic, meaning one audio channel.

Mosaic - The original Web browser program, no longer in use.

MOV - A QuickTime video file.

MP3 - A compressed audio file format used widely on the Internet. Stands for MPEG-1, Level 3.

MP3.com - A prominent music Web site hosting thousands of pages and audio files from different bands and artists.

MPEG - A data compression standard devised by the Moving Picture Experts Group. MP3 is a part of the overall MPEG standard. MPEG video file names have the extension .mpg.

Napster - The original MP3 file sharing program.

Nav (or Nav Bar) - A navigation element in a Web page, allowing you to easily view other pages within the site.

Net - An abbreviation for the Internet.

Netiquette - Etiquette on the Internet. The rules of online behavior.

Netscape Navigator - The first popular World Wide Web browser program.

newbie - An Internet beginner.

newsgroup - A Usenet discussion group (see Usenet).

newsreader - A program used to read Usenet newsgroups. Most Web browser programs contain a newsreader.

online - You're online when your computer is connected to the Internet, a BBS or an online service.

Online Service - A private network that offers Internet access and proprietary content to its members. These services include America Online and the Microsoft Network. Distinguished from ISPs, which provide primarily access.

Outlook - An e-mail program made by Microsoft.

P2P - Peer-to-Peer (see below).

Peer-to-Peer - A networking model that gives each computer both client and server capabilities. Has come to refer to applications that enable file sharing over the Net, such as Napster, Gnutella or Morpheus.

player - Software used to play back a compressed audio or video file.

plug-ins - Small programs that can be added to other programs, mainly used to enhance their multimedia capabilities. Web browsers accept plug-ins, as do many MP3 players and most professional audio editing software.

post - To send a e-mail message to a mailing list, or to add a message to a Usenet newsgroup.

PPP - Point-to-Point Protocol. A protocol (language) for Internet connection via modem, used for e-mail.

protocol - Any method (language) allowing two computers to communicate.

QuickTime - A video file format developed by Apple. QuickTime movies have a .mov file extension.

RealAudio - A compressed audio format developed by RealNetworks, commonly used for streaming.

Registrar - A firm that can assign Second-Level Domains and thereby provide you with a Web address (URL). Registrars are coordinated by ICANN, the firm that administers Internet addresses.

rip - Short for "rip-off"; it's a slang term for encoding a CD track into a compressed audio format such as MP3.

SD2 - Sound Designer II, an uncompressed audio file format for Macintosh developed by Digidesign.

SDK - Software Development Kit. Instructions and tools used by programmers to implement a licensed technology.

Search Engine - A Web site used to search the Internet for information such as names, subjects, etc.

server - The software on a host computer that allows Internet users to access it. Also used to refer to the actual host computer.

shareware - Software available on the Internet that you can download and test drive. If you like it, you can register or pay for it.

shopping cart - An e-commerce Web page that represents the customer's list of intended purchases.

signature - A text file that is automatically attached to the end of e-mail messages that contains your name and any other information you routinely share (your Web site URL, snail mail address, witty slogan, etc).

SIT file - A type of compressed data file used on Macintoshes.

site - An Internet host computer that allows some sort of access via the Internet, like a Web site or FTP site.

SLIP - Serial Line Internet Protocol. Similar to PPP, it's a way to connect to the Internet via a modem.

SMTP - Simple Mail Transfer Protocol. It's a way to transfer e-mail, used for outgoing messages.

snail mail - Internet term for conventional surface mail.

Spam - Junk newsgroup postings or unsolicited e-mail. Spamming is the act of sending unsolicited junk mail or postings.

stereo - Short for stereophonic, meaning two audio channels.

stream - To play an audio or video file over the Internet so that the user can hear or see the content as it downloads.

subscribe - To join a mailing list or start reading a Usenet newsgroup.

surf (as in surfing the Net) - To browse the World Wide Web.

tags - HTML coding statements. Also refers to metadata labels on compressed audio files, such as ID3 tags in an MP3 file.

TrueSound - An obsolete Microsoft streaming audio format.

upload - To transfer a file from your computer to another computer.

URL - Uniform Resource Locator. The natural language address of a Web page or site. For example, http://www.nameofsite.com. See also IP address, DNS.

URL scripts - Web addresses that have been inserted into a compressed audio file, such as a WMA. When the file is played the script is executed, displaying the URL in a Web browser.

Usenet - A group of computers and networks that hosts discussion groups and news articles.

VOC - Creative SoundBlaster audio format.

WAV - Microsoft's Wave, an uncompressed audio format.

Web browser - A program that displays Web pages.

webcast - To stream an audio or video presentation over the Internet live, as it is happening.

WMA - Windows Media Audio, a compressed audio file format created by Microsoft.

World Wide Web - A network of linked HTML documents on computers all over the world.

Zip file - A type of compressed data file used on PCs.

Index

A2B Music, 30
AC3, 30
acronyms, 19
Adobe GoLive, 36
Affiliate Programs, 58–59
AIFF files, 24, 25, 28, 43
Akamai, 48
AllCast, 48
Amazon.com, 59
America Online (AOL), 14–15, 18, 22,
    23, 36–37, 51
Angry Coffee, 34
Apple iTunes, 29, 31
applets, 41
archiving, 47
ASX files, 30, 44–45
ATRAC3, 30

band sites, 32–34, 57
BCC (blind carbon copy), 16–17, 69
BearShare, 52, 56
bit rate, 28
Bookmarks, 65
BPS (bits per second), 12
broadband, 12–13, 15, 37, 41, 55
browsers, Web, 10, 15, 20–21, 35, 41,
    43, 65
  e-mail programs, 16
  FTP capabilities, 11
bulletin board services, 10

cable modems, 12–13, 15, 55
carbon copy functions, 16–17, 69
CBR/VBR, 29
CC (carbon copy), 16–17, 69
CCNOW, 61
CD manufacturing, 63
CDDB, 67
CDNOW, 59
CenterSpan, 52
Chat, 14, 22–23
ClickBank, 59

client-server network, 50
codecs, 27, 29–31
compression, audio file, 24, 27–31, 33,
     40, 43, 47, 58–59
computer viruses, 52
computers, 12
content delivery networks, 48
Cool Edit 2000, 25
copyright issues, 30, 50, 53, 62
cover versions, 33
cropping, 26

D.A.M. CDs, 58
DC offset, 26
DejaNews Usenet archive, 19
dial-up connections, 12, 14, 15, 28,
     41, 43, 55
DigiBuy, 62
Digital Island, 48
digitizing music, 24–26
Discmakers, 63
discussion groups, 14
DNS (Domain Name System), 40, 42
Dogpile, 21
domain names, registering, 42
download times, 13, 55
downloadable audio files, 24–26, 40
   adding URLs to, 70–71
   selling, 61–62
Download.com, 56
DRM (Digital Rights Management), 30,
     31, 61–62
DSL (Digital Subscriber Line), 13, 15,
     46, 55

e-mail, 9, 16–17, 72
   addresses, 16, 68–69
   file attachments, 17
   mailing lists and, 11
   online services, 14
   signatures, 69
   software, 16, 20
   solicited vs. Spam, 17
emoticons, 17
encoders, 24–25, 27, 29, 30, 31, 45–46
ePAC, 30
equalization, 26

Fanning, Shawn, 50
FastTrack, 52
Fetch, 11, 37
file compression. See compression,
    audio file
file names, 54–55
file sharing, 48, 49–56, 72
  basics of, 49–50
    decisions on, 53
    schemes, 50–52
    second-generation, 52–53
files, audio, 24–25, 28, 43, 70–71. See
    also specific types
fixed wireless connections, 13
Flash, 41
folders, computer file, 37–38, 49–50,
    52, 55–56
frames, 39
Frankel, Justin, 51
Fraunhofer Institute, 29, 31
FTP address, 37
FTP client program, 11, 37
FTP (File Transfer Protocol), 11, 20,
    44
FTP Voyager, 11, 37

Garageband Records, 32
GIF files, 33, 39
GigAmerica, 32
Gnutella, 51–52, 56
Google, 21
Google Groups, 19
graphics files, 33
Guerrilla Marketing Handbook, The, 71

hierarchies, Usenet, 18
home page, 7, 37, 38, 65
host computers, 10, 16, 36–37, 46–47,
    50, 55–56
HTML editors, 36, 69
HTML (Hypertext Markup Language), 10,
    35–36, 40, 66, 69
HTML Meta Tags, 65–67
HTTP streaming, 45–46
hyper-links, 44

iBeam, 48
ICQ, 23
ID3v1 and ID3v2, 30, 70–71
importing music, 24–25
Instant Messaging, 14, 23
Internet
  accessing, 14–15
  advantages of, 7–8
  basics of, 9–11
  equipment requirements for, 12–13
  terminology, 11
Internet radio, 47–48
InterNIC, 42
InterTrust, 62
IP address, 15, 40
IRC (Internet Relay Chat), 22–23
Ircle, 22–23
ISDN, 12
ISP (Internet Service Provider), 14–15,
    16, 18, 36, 46–47, 53, 55
IUMA, 32, 57

Java, 41
joint stereo, 29
JPEG files, 33, 39

keywords, 66

L1, 26
LimeWire, 51, 52, 56
limiting, 26
links, 10, 40, 70
Liquid Audio, 30, 62
live webcasting, 46–47
Live365, 47, 48
Local Area Networks, 49–50
lurking, 18

M3U files, 30, 44
Macintosh computer, 12, 24, 41, 49
mailing lists, 9, 11, 16–17, 19, 68–69
masking, 27
MediaForce, 53
merchant services, 61
Metadata. See tags
metrics, 64

Microsoft FrontPage, 36
Microsoft Internet Explorer, 10, 11,
    20–21, 41, 43, 65
Microsoft Network, 14, 22, 23
Microsoft Outlook and Outlook Express,
    16, 17
Microsoft Windows Media Rights Manager,
    62
mIRC, 22–23
M.I.R.V. (band), 7
modems, 12–13, 28
mono audio files, 26, 28–29, 45
Morpheus, 52
MP3 files, 24, 27, 29–30, 31, 33–34, 40
    download times for, 13, 55
    enhancing, 71
    sharing, 50–55
    streaming, 43, 44
    uploading, 48
MP3.com, 32, 57–58, 64
mp3PRO, 31
MusicMatch Jukebox, 29, 31, 43
MyHitLogger, 64

Napster, 50–51
navigation bars, 39
NEATO system, 63
NetPD, 53
Netscape Composer, 36
Netscape Navigator, 10, 11, 16, 20–21,
    41, 43, 65
newsgroups, 10–11, 17, 18–19
newsreaders, 10, 18, 20
normalizing, 26

offline promotion, 71
Ogg Vorbis, 31
online services, 14–15, 16, 18, 22
online stores, 59–61

page-view counters, 64
pages, Web, 7, 10
"payback for playback," 57
PayPal, 61
Peak, 25
Peer-to-Peer networks, 48, 49, 50–51,
    53, 54–56, 70, 72

perceptual coding, 27–28
players, 24–25, 27, 29, 30, 43, 45, 51
PPP server, 15
Pro Tools, 25

QuickTime, 40, 43

RAM, 12
RealAudio, 45–46
RealJukebox, 31
RealMedia format, 45
RealNetworks, 48
RealProducer, 45, 46–47
RealSystem Server, 46
record label, creating your own, 63
reflectors, 52
Releasing an Independent Record, 63
replicators, 63
reporting, 64
rip, 27
royalties, 57

satellite DSL services, 13
Scrub The Web, 67
SD2 files, 24, 25, 28, 43
search engines, 8, 20, 21, 66
   submitting sites to, 41, 67–68
selling music online, 57–63
servers, 10, 46, 50
ShareSniffer, 52–53
shopping carts, 60, 61
SHOUTcast, 44, 47
silence, inserting, 26
SMTP server, 15
sound cards, 25
sound-editing software, 24–26
Sound Forge, 24, 25
Sound Studio, 25
Spam, 17, 55, 69
Spinner, 47
stereo audio files, 26, 28–29
streaming audio, 24, 28, 30, 31, 40,
   43–47
Stuffit, 27
SureStream, 46
surfing, Web, 20, 37

T-1 and T-3 lines, 13, 46
tags, 28, 30, 54–55, 70–71. See also
     HTML Meta Tags
Terms of Service, 34, 55
top level domain designation, 16
TTL (Time To Live), 56

"under construction," 41
uploading, 33–34, 44, 45, 48
URL addresses, 20, 34, 37, 40, 44, 54,
     69
   submitting, 41, 67–68
URL scripts, 30, 70–71
Usenet, 10–11, 17, 18–19, 36, 50

Vitaminic, 32, 57
Vivendi-Universal, 32

WAV files, 24, 25, 28, 43, 71
Web consultants, 42
Web page analyzers, 67
Web Rings, 0
Web sites, 7, 21, 72
   aggregate band sites, 32–34, 57
   applets on, 41
   audio downloads, 40, 61–62, 72
   building traffic, 64–71
   creating your own, 8, 10, 35–42, 72
   information included on, 33–34, 38
   navigation on, 39
   provided by online services, 14–15
WebTrends Live, 65
Windows Media Encoder, 30, 46–47, 70–71
Windows Media Player, 30, 31, 43, 45,
     71
Windows PC, 12, 24, 41, 49
WinRip Studio, 71
Winzip, 27
WMA files, 27, 30, 31, 40, 71
   enhancing, 70–71
   sharing, 54
   streaming, 43, 44–45
World Wide Web, 10, 14, 20–21

Yahoo!, 20, 21, 67–68